THE ADVENTURES OF SHERLOCK HOLMES

Detecting Social Order

Rosemary Jann

TWAYNE PUBLISHERS • NEW YORK
Maxwell Macmillan Canada • *Toronto*
Maxwell Macmillan International • *New York Oxford Singapore Sydney*

Twayne's Masterwork Series No. 152

The Adventures of Sherlock Holmes: Detecting Social Order
Rosemary Jann

Twayne Publishers   Maxwell Macmillan Canada, Inc.
Macmillan Publishing Company   1200 Eglinton Avenue East
866 Third Avenue   Suite 200
New York, New York 10022   Don Mills, Ontario M3C 3N1

Library of Congress Cataloging-in-Publication Data

Jann, Rosemary, 1949–
    The adventures of Sherlock Holmes : detecting social order / Rosemary Jann.
        p. cm.—(Twayne's masterwork studies ; no. 152)
    Includes bibliographical references and index.
    ISBN 0-8057-8384-9 (cloth). — ISBN 0-8057-8385-7 (ppr)
    1. Doyle, Arthur Conan, Sir, 1859–1930—Characters—Sherlock Holmes.
    2. Detective and mystery stories, English—History and criticism.   3. Holmes,
    Sherlock (Fictitious character)   4. Private investigators in literature.   5. Social
    norms in literature.   6. Literature and society.   I. Title.   II. Series.
    PR4624.J35   1995
    823'.8—dc20   94-32326
                                                                          CIP

The paper used in this publication meets the minimum requirements of American National Standard for Information Sciences—Permanence of Paper for Printed Library Materials. ANSI Z3948–1984. ∞™

10 9 8 7 6 5 4 3 2 1 (hc)
10 9 8 7 6 5 4 3 2 1 (pb)

Printed in the United States of America

No mystery: for Scott

Contents

List of Illustrations

Arthur Conan Doyle, about 1904.

Reproduced courtesy of the Lancelyn Green Collection.

Note on the References and Acknowledgments

Because I have drawn evidence from throughout the Sherlock Holmes canon, I have chosen to use the 1986 Bantam two-volume paperback *Sherlock Holmes: The Complete Novels and Stories* as my reference text, cited by volume and page thus: 1:432. The Bantam is based on the standard American edition, the Doubleday (1930), which differs in minor ways from the standard English editions by John Murray (1928–29). To facilitate the location of citations in the many other available editions of the Sherlock Holmes stories, I have also included abbreviated story titles in my references, following those used by Jack Tracy in *The Encyclopedia Sherlockiana* (xix).

BERY: "Beryl Coronet"
BLUE: "Blue Carbuncle"
BOSC: "Boscombe Valley Mystery"
BRUC: "Bruce-Partington Plans"
CHAS: "Charles Augustus Milverton"
COPP: "Copper Beeches"
CREE: "Creeping Man"
CROO: "Crooked Man"
DEVI: "Devil's Foot"
DYIN: "Dying Detective"
EMPT: "Empty House"
ENGR: "Engineer's Thumb"
FINA: "Final Solution"

FIVE: "Five Orange Pips"
GOLD: "Golden Pince-Nez"
GREE: "Greek Interpreter"
HOUN: "Hound of the Baskervilles"
IDEN: "Case of Identity"
ILLU: "Illustrious Client"
LADY: "Lady Frances Carfax"
NAVA: "Naval Treaty"
NOBL: "Noble Bachelor"
NORW: "Norwood Builder"
REDC: "Red Circle"
REDH: "Red-Headed League"
REIG: "Reigate Puzzle"
SCAN: "Scandal in Bohemia"
SECO: "Second Stain"
SHOS: "Shoscombe Old Place"
SIGN: "Sign of Four"
SILV: "Silver Blaze"
SOLI: "Solitary Cyclist"
SPEC: "Speckled Band"
STUD: "Study in Scarlet"
THOR: "Thor Bridge"
3GAR: "Three Garridebs"
TWIS: "Man with the Twisted Lip"
VALL: "Valley of Fear"
WIST: "Wisteria Lodge"

I am grateful to Victoria Gill of the Metropolitan Toronto Reference Library for her assistance in securing reproductions of the Sidney Paget illustrations from "The Boscombe Valley Mystery" and "The Blue Carbuncle" and to Richard Lancelyn Green for kindly allowing me to use the frontispiece portrait of Arthur Conan Doyle. I would also extend my gratitude to Johns Hopkins University Press for granting me permission to use parts of my essay "Sherlock Holmes Codes the Social Body," which originally appeared in *English Literary History* 57 (1990): 685–708.

Note on the References and Acknowledgments

Thanks are also in order to my colleagues Deborah Kaplan, Devon Hodges, and Eileen Sypher, who offered helpful comments at various stages of this project, and to the Faculty Study Leave program at George Mason University, which made possible its timely completion. For his unfailing love and support, I dedicate this book to my husband, Scott Keeter.

Chronology: Arthur Conan Doyle's Life and Work

1859	Born at 11 Picardy Place, Edinburgh, on 22 May, the second child and eldest son of Charles Altamont Doyle and Mary Foley Doyle. Because his father, an architect and painter, is rendered largely ineffectual by epilepsy and alcoholism, Arthur is most strongly influenced and supported by his mother, who encourages in him a love of literature and history and a romanticized pride in their noble ancestry. Arthur, like his older sister, Annette, takes the name Conan Doyle after their childless granduncle, Michael Conan.
1868	Enters Hodder, a Roman Catholic preparatory school for Stonyhurst in Lancashire. Distinguishes himself early as a storyteller and an athlete.
1870	Enters Stonyhurst, the Jesuit college, and thereafter spends five years under strict discipline and Spartan conditions.
1875	Not yet ready to choose a career, Doyle attends Feldkirch, a Jesuit school in Austria, for a year at the recommendation of his teachers.
1876	Begins study at Edinburgh University's Faculty of Medicine, where he meets Joseph Bell, a surgeon whom he studied with and worked for and who would later become the most important model for Sherlock Holmes. While a medical student, begins writing to supplement his meager income.
1879	Publishes his first short story, "The Mystery of Sasassa Valley," in the October *Chambers's Journal*.
1880	Travels to the Arctic as a ship's doctor on a whaling boat.
1881	Receives Bachelor of Medicine degree.

1882	Deprived of assistance from his Roman Catholic relatives by his retreat into agnosticism, he must fend for himself in starting his career. He briefly joins a partnership with George Budd in Plymouth, and then, after a falling out, establishes himself in private practice in Southsea, Portsmouth.
1884	The January *Cornhill Magazine* publishes "J. Habakuk Jephson's Statement," a fictionalized account of a mysterious abandoned ship so realistic that some readers mistake it as purporting to be factual.
1885	Marries Louise ("Touie") Hawkins, after a brief courtship; theirs will be a union based more on affection and respect than on passion. Completes his first novel, *The Firm of Girdlestone*, based in part on his Edinburgh experiences, but does not succeed in publishing it until 1890.
1886	Completes *A Study in Scarlet*, the first Sherlock Holmes fiction, and Ward, Lock, and Company eventually agree to buy the copyright for the small sum of £25.
1887	Publishes *A Study in Scarlet* in *Beeton's Christmas Annual*, where it is moderately successful and is reprinted as a separate work in 1888.
1889	First daughter, Mary Louise, born in January. Doyle publishes *Micah Clarke*, a historical novel concerning seventeenth-century English Puritans.
1890	Publishes *The Sign of Four*, the second Sherlock Holmes fiction, in May in the American *Lippincott's Magazine*.
1891	Publishes *The White Company*, a historical novel set in the chivalric world of the fourteenth century. Studies ophthalmology in Vienna; returns to London to set himself up as a specialist, but shortly afterward decides to give up medicine for writing full-time. Publishes the first six of what would become *The Adventures of Sherlock Holmes* in the *Strand Magazine* between July and December.
1892	Publishes the second six stories of the *Adventures* in the *Strand* between January and June, and "Silver Blaze" in December. Birth of a son, Alleyne Kingsley, in November.
1893	Doyle publishes the rest of the stories that will make up *The Memoirs of Sherlock Holmes* in the *Strand*, with Holmes apparently killed off in December's "The Final Problem." Publishes *The Refugees*, a historical fiction based on Huguenots in France and Canada. After Louise is diagnosed with tuberculosis, departs with his family for several years abroad in

Chronology

search of a better climate for her. Death of Charles Altamont Doyle.

1894   Doyle begins to serialize *The Stark Munro Letters*, a fictionalized version of his own earlier struggles with religious doubt. Tours the United States between October and December.

1895   Serializes in the *Strand* the stories that he will publish the following year as *The Exploits of Brigadier Gerard*, the first of several historical fictions based in the Napoleonic era and celebrating the adventures of a French soldier.

1896   Returns with family to England to live eventually at Hindhead in Surrey. Publishes *Rodney Stone*, set in the prizefighting circles of the English Regency period.

1897   Publishes *Uncle Bernac*, a historical fiction set in France and featuring Napoleon as a protagonist. Meets and falls in love with Jean Leckie, with whom he maintains an intense but platonic relationship until his wife's death.

1898   Publishes *The Tragedy of the Korosko*, an adventure set in contemporary Egypt.

1899   Publishes the modern love story *A Duet, with an Occasional Chorus*. The American actor William Gillette, with Doyle's blessing, writes and stars in a very successful play based on the adventures of Sherlock Holmes, which would go on to numerous performances and revivals in later years.

1900   Doyle publishes *The Great Boer War*, an analysis of the issues leading up to the conflict. Serves for several months at Bloemfontein Field Hospital in South Africa. Stands unsuccessfully as a Liberal Unionist candidate for Parliament.

1901   Begins serialization of *The Hound of the Baskervilles* in the *Strand*, to be concluded the following April.

1902   Publishes *The War in South Africa: Its Cause and Conduct*. Is knighted on 9 August.

1903–1904   Resuscitates Holmes in "The Empty House," in the September *Strand*. Issues the remaining stories that will compose *The Return of Sherlock Holmes* until December 1904. Also publishes a second series of Brigadier Gerard stories, *Adventures of Gerard*, in 1903.

1906   Louise dies on 4 July. Doyle again defeated for Parliament. Publishes *Sir Nigel*, another chivalric novel expanding on the earlier life of a character from *The White Company*. Becomes involved in investigating the case of George Edalji, whom he believed to be wrongly accused of mutilating cattle.

1907	Marries Jean Leckie, 18 September. Their family home becomes Windlesham in Sussex. Publishes *Through the Magic Door*, his musings on his favorite books.
1908–1917	Most of the Sherlock Holmes stories constituting *His Last Bow* appear in the *Strand*.
1909	A son, Denis Percy Stewart, born in March. Doyle publishes "The Crime of the Congo," exposing Belgian abuses in Africa, and "Divorce Law Reform: An Essay."
1910	A son, Adrian Malcolm, born in November. Doyle becomes involved in investigating the case of Oscar Slater, who, he believed, was wrongly accused of murder, and persists until Slater's release was finally secured in 1927.
1912	A daughter, Jean Lena Annette, born in December. Publishes *The Lost World*, the first of the tales featuring the eccentric Professor Challenger.
1913	Publishes a second Challenger fiction, *The Poison Belt*. Tries to arouse British concern about the German threat in "Great Britain and the Next War."
1914	Tries unsuccessfully to enlist when war is declared on 4 August and plays an important role in civil defense at home.
1914–1915	Serializes a short Sherlock Holmes novel, *The Valley of Fear*, in the *Strand*.
1916	Publishes the first volume of his six-volume history *The British Campaign in France and Flanders*.
1918	His son Kingsley dies of influenza while recuperating from war injuries. Doyle publishes *The New Revelation*, announcing his conversion to spiritualism.
1919	Publishes *The Vital Message*, another spiritualist work. Begins several years of extensive lecturing in England and abroad on spiritualist topics. Death of his brother Innes.
1921	Doyle publishes *Wanderings of a Spiritualist*. His mother dies.
1921–1927	Doyle publishes the final stories making up *The Casebook of Sherlock Holmes* in the *Strand*, concluding with "Shoscombe Old Place" in April 1927.
1922	Undermines his credibility by publishing *The Coming of the Fairies*, in which he endorses faked photographs purporting to prove the existence of fairies.
1924	Publishes his autobiography, *Memories and Adventures*.
1925	Begins serialization of *The Land of Mist*, in which Professor Challenger converts to a belief in spiritualism.

Chronology

1926   Publishes his two-volume *History of Spiritualism*.

1930   Dies on 7 July of a heart attack at home in Windlesham, Surrey.

LITERARY AND
HISTORICAL CONTEXT

1

The Last Victorian Hero

From the detective's introduction in the 1887 novel *A Study in Scarlet* to his final adventures collected in the *Casebook* of 1927, the publication history of Sherlock Holmes spanned a 40-year period. In setting as well as in spirit, however, the Holmes saga created by Sir Arthur Conan Doyle is quintessentially late Victorian. Two-thirds of the 60 Sherlock Holmes tales were published by 1903, and the vast majority are set in the closing decades of the reign of Queen Victoria (1837–1901).[1] They serve as both culmination to, and commentary on, the dominant cultural trends of the Victorian period. The all but invincible Sherlock Holmes was the suitable heir to a century in which England's successes in industrialization and empire made it the most powerful country in the world.

Perhaps most significant to his appeal were the ways in which his brilliant ratiocination celebrated the accomplishments of science in the age of Charles Darwin. As breakthroughs in geology and evolutionary biology challenged the adequacy of the older, biblical worldview during this period, science offered the alternative certainty of a world whose order was subject to law and accessible to human reason. Holmes's ability to "read" the human body drew confidence from the many biological typologies developed during the nineteenth century to identify and systematize the signs of human difference. The detective's reconstruction of the crime shared significant common ground with contemporary methods used to reconstruct the past, as Victorian scientist Thomas Henry Huxley pointed out in his suggestively titled 1880 essay "The Method of Zadig: Retrospective Prophecy as a Function of Science."[2] Borrowing his title from Voltaire's character Zadig, who is accused of theft after he correctly describes a horse and dog he had never seen by interpreting the signs they had left behind, Huxley argued that the foundation of natural science rests on the imaginative ability to reconstruct from present clues what was past or absent; this process empowered the paleontologist who extrapolated an entire organism from fossil fragments, as well as the Darwin who posited causes operating in the past to account for the shape of present order. Sherlock Holmes draws on this analogy himself in "The Five Orange Pips": just as the famous French anatomist Georges Cuvier "could correctly describe a whole animal by the contemplation of a single bone, so the observer who has thoroughly understood one link in a series of incidents should be able to accurately state all the other ones, both before and after" (1:300). Through the character of Holmes, Doyle brilliantly popularized the century's confidence in the uniform operation of scientific laws that allowed the trained observer to deduce causes from effects and what had passed from clues left behind. In the process, he offered a powerful image of the scientist as hero, to counter the arrogance of the Victor Frankensteins and Dr. Jekylls of nineteenth-century fiction.[3]

Although the fixation in much Sherlock Holmes criticism on explicit parallels between the lives of author and character has at times hindered our appreciation of Doyle's creative talents, it is useful to consider ways in which his values and experiences were imaginatively transmuted in the character of Holmes and his other literary creations. Sir Arthur Conan Doyle in many ways fulfilled the model of the Victorian gentleman: an avid adventurer, sportsman, and patriot, he was a living embodiment of Victorian ideals of manliness, gallantry, and self-reliance. The romantic code of chivalric honor and noblesse oblige instilled in him by his mother informed his own behavior as well as that of the heroes he created for historical novels like *The White Company* and *Sir Nigel*. Holmes is one of many updated versions in the Doyle canon of the hero who unselfishly enlists his talents in a quest for truth and justice, much as did Doyle himself as a tireless publicist for numerous political and social causes. That this new knight-errant arms himself with rationality is also biographically significant. Like so many Victorians, Doyle underwent a crisis of faith that painfully alienated him from some family members. He retreated into agnosticism when the unquestioning religious faith of his childhood was found lacking by the standards of scientific proof that had informed his training as a medical doctor. Scientific heroes like Holmes and like Professor Challenger in *The Lost World* and other romances offered Conan Doyle an important means of valorizing the choices that he felt his "scientific desire for truth" and his "intellectual self-respect" had forced him to make.[4]

The Holmes character validated Doyle's personal choices in another respect. As the middle classes gained in economic and political power during the nineteenth century, they consolidated their cultural authority by remodeling the definition of the gentleman. True gentility was progressively redefined to stress traits of mind and character rather than inherited wealth and lineage, and the right to cultural leadership came to depend more on an aristocracy of talent than on one of birth. Holmes, the disinterested intellectual in the service of society who accepts remuneration for his work but does not require it, offers an interesting late Victorian validation of this new kind of culture hero—the gentleman who lives by his wits, not unlike the genteel but poor young Arthur Conan Doyle, who initially had to struggle to earn his living first as a doctor and then as a writer after his split with his Roman Catholic relatives deprived him of the benefits of their wealth and influence. The immense prestige Holmes earns not by any kind of vulgar self-aggrandizement but by the pursuit of a highly intellectualized "art" must have been peculiarly reassuring not just to Doyle himself but also to the middle-class readers of the *Strand Magazine* who made Holmes an overnight sensation in the early 1890s. Doyle's ambivalence about Holmes is also easier to understand when considered in this context. He repeatedly resisted calls for more Holmes stories, in part because of the effort involved in fabricating adequate plots but also because he feared that their very success threatened to identify him entirely with what he "regarded as a lower stratum of literary achievement" (M&A, 93). The fact that he several times gave in after being offered increasingly larger sums of money for more Holmes stories left his professional identity split between the gentleman of letters, disinterestedly devoted to higher art forms like the historical novel, and the rather more businesslike writer who became rich from rapidly turned-out popular fiction.

If Sherlock Holmes can be seen as a kind of modern epic hero summarizing the most valued traits of his class and era, we should also consider Pasquale Accardo's judgment that "the epic that epitomizes any given age is written when that age is nearing its end, when its carefully realized ethos is seriously threatened by decay and conflict from within."[5] Holmes was also a creation of the fin de siècle, that "end of the century" period overshadowed by fears of cultural decadence and increasing fragmentation. Although in his early appearances Holmes sports some traits reminiscent of the dandies and aesthetes of the decadent 1890s, his eccentricities never really endanger his social position or function. Among contemporaries unsettled by fears of cultural disintegration, he surely owed much of his popularity to the reassurance offered them by the reiterated spectacle of successful detections, dangers contained, order restored, and values reaffirmed. As readers in Doyle's own lifetime moved forward into the mounting uncertainties of the twentieth century, they could still turn to the earlier and increasingly nostalgia-inducing London of the Holmes stories, in which it is always late in the reign of Victoria and Sherlock Holmes and John Watson stand always ready to brave the dangers of a world that contains no problems inaccessible to the intelligence and energy of brave men. The increasing complexity of our own social problems has done little to lessen, and much to increase, the satisfactions of the Holmes formula. In exploring the adventures of the world's most famous detective, we will also be exploring our own desire for a transcendent moral order confirmed by justice and reason and for a society in which power naturally corresponds with virtue.

2

The Holmes Phenomenon

Sherlock Holmes is one of the very few literary figures who can be said to have attained the status of myth. He has worldwide name recognition, even among millions who have never read the original sources. Indeed, the name is scarcely necessary: the famous silhouette, with deerstalker cap, meerschaum pipe, and aquiline profile, and the tag line "Elementary, my dear Watson!" are enough to conjure him up in the imagination. Since his inception, he has inspired countless pastiches, parodies, and adaptations in various media and many languages; he is the subject of fan clubs worldwide. He was assumed by many to be a real person in the 1890s and continues to attract a more or less playful cult of writers who treat his adventures as history rather than fiction. This phenomenal popularity alone would justify sending us back to the texts that inspired it and shaped an entire genre of detective fiction in early twentieth-century England.

Holmes's initial success with readers was due at least in part to Doyle's early mastery of magazine serialization at a time of expanding readership. The detective leapt into the public imagination in late 1891, after the first of the 12 short stories that make up *The Adventures of Sherlock Holmes* began to appear in the then-new *Strand Magazine*.

"We had the Carriage to Ourselves": Original Sidney Paget illustration for "The Boscombe Valley Mystery."

Reproduced courtesy of the Metropolitan Toronto Reference Library.

Less expensive, more widely marketed, and less intellectually demanding than the older Victorian monthlies, the *Strand* was aimed at a middle-class family audience seeking information and entertainment.[1] Doyle realized the advantages of a series of self-contained stories featuring the same character over a novel serialized in monthly parts when it came to "binding readers to a particular magazine" (M&A, 90): whereas missing one monthly installment of a serialized work might cause readers to lose interest, a series of stories depended less on sequential reading than on a protagonist sufficiently attractive to keep readers buying the magazine that offered his latest set of adventures— a role the brilliant and eccentric Holmes ably filled. Doyle rightly credited himself with being the first to master a formula that has since become a familiar part of popular fiction.

As the detective's trademark appearance and expressions might suggest, the creation of Holmes in all his imaginative immediacy was a collaborative affair. Sidney Paget substituted his more handsome brother Walter as a model for the rather gaunt and ugly Sherlock of Doyle's initial conception when drafting the original *Strand* illustrations of the *Adventures*. These widely reproduced drawings gave Holmes the hat, pipe, and well-bred suavity that first defined the detective's image in the public mind. This image was further elaborated by the American actor William Gillette, who, with Doyle's blessing, created a hit play based on the Holmes stories, a play that kept Gillette as the embodiment of Holmes on American and British stages for many years following its opening night in 1899. Gillette, in turn, served as model for Frederic Dorr Steele's elegant illustrations of the later Holmes stories in the American magazine *Collier's Weekly*.[2] Since then, dozens more stage, screen, and radio Holmeses have empowered the character with a life of his own. The familiar line "Elementary, my dear Watson," for instance, does not appear in Doyle; it may have derived from words Gillette used on the stage and probably gained currency as the dramatic curtain line of a popular radio version of the Gillette play adapted by Orson Welles in the late 1930s.[3]

Although Doyle sometimes professed amazement or annoyance at the public's tendency to treat Holmes as an actual person, it is a rare compliment to his skill that he could make characters so imaginatively credible as to transcend the boundaries of fiction. The stories possess an air of factuality that deliberately fostered this impression. Watson's tantalizing allusions to other cases he might someday write about and his casual assurance that his audience is already familiar with many of these from the public press,[4] playfully insinuate the reader's participation in this fictional world. The specificity of Doyle's settings made them instantly recognizable to a contemporary reader and enhanced the illusion of realism. Doyle's true heart belonged to historical fiction, but perhaps he did not appreciate how intensely the same powerful historical imagination and sense of place that shaped the imaginary pasts he had so lovingly constructed for the Puritan England of *Micah Clarke* or the Napoleonic France of *The Exploits of Brigadier Gerard* also informed the London of the Sherlock Holmes stories. This effect depends on more than the simple use of props, like mentioning actual train stations and parts of town or summoning up the characteristic pea-soup fogs and gaslights of later Victorian London. Doyle had mastered the art of creating what Howard Haycraft called a "romantic reality":[5] the ability to capture the feeling and not just the surface of place, to envelop the reader in atmosphere with a few emotive details. Although the continued vitality of the Sherlock Holmes stories owes much to the fascination of the Holmes character and to the sheer puzzle-solving pleasure generated by Doyle's deft plotting, perhaps the greatest tribute to Doyle's skill as a writer lies in this ability to create a landscape of the imagination more compelling than the real thing, to give definitive shape to a time and place in the minds of millions. The power of literature resides in its ability to create places and characters that live beyond the perishable present and can thus become the shared property of generations of readers; preeminent among them is the phenomenon known as Sherlock Holmes.

3

One Hundred Years of Holmes and the Critics

Somewhat surprisingly, given his later popularity, the career of Sherlock Holmes got off to an inauspicious start. Struggling to supplement his physician's income with his pen, Arthur Conan Doyle resolved to try his hand at the kind of detective story that Edgar Allan Poe in the United States and Émile Gaboriau in France had pioneered. He offered the result, a short novel entitled *A Study in Scarlet*, to several publishers before Ward, Lock, and Company finally accepted it, and then only on the condition that they wait a year to bring it out in *Beeton's Christmas Annual* for 1887, since the market was "flooded at the present with cheap fiction."[1] Doyle's tale attracted enough attention to be reprinted independently in 1888. When the American publishers of *Lippincott's Magazine* invited Doyle to contribute a long piece of fiction, he used Holmes again in *The Sign of Four*, which appeared in February 1890 to a warmer welcome.[2]

The real success of Sherlock Holmes, however, dates from his first appearance in the *Strand Magazine*, to which Doyle had offered two short stories featuring the detective in 1891. In this popular format, Doyle's intriguing characterization and ingenious plotting made Holmes a sensation soon after the appearance of "A Scandal in

Bohemia" in the July issue. He had originally intended to write only six stories, but by October, he wrote to his mother, "The *Strand* are simply imploring me to continue Sherlock Holmes."[3] It was difficult, he found, to "spin" out the kind of "clearcut and original" plots he demanded of himself; produced at such a rate, they were "apt to become thin or break" (M&A, 92), not to mention how hard it was to take time away from what he considered more serious literary work.

When increasing his fee per story did not dampen the *Strand*'s enthusiasm, he considered killing off Sherlock Holmes at the end of the first 12 stories, published in book form as *The Adventures of Sherlock Holmes* in 1892, only to be dissuaded by his mother. He finally made good on this threat in December 1893. At the end of the twenty-fourth story, "The Final Problem," Holmes disappears at the brink of Switzerland's Reichenbach Falls with his mortal enemy, Professor Moriarty. (This second series of stories, minus "The Cardboard Box," was published as *The Memoirs of Sherlock Holmes* in 1894). Although Doyle decided rather as an afterthought to use the Holmes character in the Gothic tale that became *The Hound of the Baskervilles* (1901–02), he set this story before Holmes's disappearance. It was not until 1903, when the American publisher Collier's made him a financial offer he could not refuse, that he agreed to resurrect the famous sleuth, whom "The Adventure of the Empty House" presents as having been in hiding for several years since he ensured Moriarty's death and faked his own at the falls in order more effectively to pursue the remaining members of Moriarty's gang. Doyle would go on to write several more series of Holmes stories (collected in book form as *The Return of Sherlock Holmes*, 1905; *His Last Bow*, 1917; and *The Casebook of Sherlock Holmes*, 1927) and one more novel featuring him (*The Valley of Fear*, 1914–15). The great detective was presumed to be still living in retirement when his creator died in 1930.

As early as *The Sign of Four*, which elicited a request from an American tobacconist for Holmes's monograph on identifying types of ash, many readers believed the vividly realized detective to be a real person. They sent accounts of cases for him to solve to Scotland Yard and Baker Street; similar requests were addressed directly to Doyle and to Joseph Bell, the Edinburgh doctor whom Doyle had identified as a model for Sherlock Holmes. Readers petitioned Doyle for Holmes's portrait, his autograph, and even locks of hair; less literal-minded ones sent suggestions for plots and objections to Doyle's claims about interpreting evidence and the law. American audiences reportedly went away disappointed that the lecturer Doyle was not, as expected, "a cadaverous looking person with marks of cocaine injections all over him."[4] Newspapers and journals greeted the news of Holmes's "death" in 1893 with headlines and dismayed farewells; London clerks wore black crape around their hats and indignant letter writers denounced Doyle as a "brute." Holmes's revival in *The Hound of the Baskervilles* was greeted by long lines at the offices of the *Strand Magazine*; one commentator described the crowds vying for copies of "The Empty House" at railway bookstalls as "worse than anything at a bargain sale." Holmes's persistent appeal helped guarantee that the name of Conan Doyle on a *Strand* cover could always be counted on to sell thousands of extra copies.[5] Holmes was still alive and well in popular memory in 1951, when a facsimile of his rooms at 221b Baker Street attracted more than 50,000 visitors during the Festival of Britain. The centenary of Holmes's supposed birth in 1954 and of that of his creator in 1959 were also marked by celebrations of his memory (Nordon, 206–7). Another Sherlock Holmes boom in the 1970s witnessed the Royal Shakespeare Company's revival of William Gillette's play and Nicholas Meyer's novel (and movie) *The Seven Per-Cent Solution* (in which Sigmund Freud treats Holmes for cocaine addiction), as well as the publication of numerous guides, handbooks, and companion studies to the fiction.

The earliest and longest-lived school of Holmesian criticism followed popular example, devoting itself to the sport of pretending that Holmes and Watson were real people and searching "the Sacred Canon" of Holmes stories for clues to the chronology and specifics of their lives and adventures. This sort of intellectual parlor game can be said to have started with an open letter to Watson requesting clarification of inconsistencies in *The Hound of the Baskervilles*, published by Frank Sidgwick in 1902. Such commentary borrowed the label "the Higher Criticism" from a school of German biblical scholarship dedicated to establishing the historical bases of scripture. Ronald Knox satirized the textual methods of this approach by applying them to Holmes's life and adventures in a 1911 essay. This inspired other scholars at Oxford and Cambridge to join the game of pretending that Arthur Conan Doyle was a mere literary agent for the real Watson, Holmes's biographer, and to imitate Holmes's own methods of deducing hidden meanings from apparently trifling details about their lives contained in the stories. With the publication of several biographies and other studies of this pair, the "Sherlockian" school was flourishing by the 1930s, when the American novelist Christopher Morley founded the Baker Street Irregulars to pursue its activities in the United States. It remains alive and well today, to be found in its most current form in the pages of the *Baker Street Journal*. Although its tireless pursuit of influences, inconsistencies, and possible sources pokes some deserved fun at certain styles of academic criticism and has shed some useful light on the historical context of the Holmes stories, too often the relentless literality of the Sherlockian approach ends ironically by impoverishing the very imaginative and literary achievements that attract most readers to the stories in the first place.[6]

More intellectually serious, but in some cases just as much focused on the search for parallels and sources, has been the early and prolonged interest in the life of Arthur Conan Doyle as the creator of Sherlock Holmes. Since his death in 1930, no fewer than 13 full-length biographies of Doyle have been published; many other biographically oriented studies of the Holmes fiction have also appeared. From the beginning, debate raged about Doyle's true character: Was he a simple "man in the street," as his early biographer Hesketh Pearson had claimed, or the larger-than-life romantic hero painted (with the blessings of Sir Arthur's son Adrian) by John Dickson Carr? Did his bluff, typically Victorian public persona reveal all there was to know, or was it a carefully cultivated blind for more complex depths? In short, was he Watson or Holmes? The choice is, of course, an artificial one. Biographers have made clear that there was certainly more than met the public eye in the private life of a man who had suffered through childhood with an alcoholic father; remained faithful to his ailing wife for more than ten years while cherishing a chaste and secret love for Jean Leckie, who would become the second Lady Conan Doyle; and became a credulous supporter of spiritualism after years as the champion of rationality and scientific standards of proof. Although Doyle's modesty more often led him to present himself as a mere Watson, he shared the photographic memory and the ability to deduce character from appearance that distinguished Sherlock Holmes and on more than one occasion used his detective skills to solve real mysteries (Nordon, 115–38, 194; M&A, 105–7). As to whether he had to "be" Holmes in order to have created him, Doyle himself offered the best reply. Psychologically, he argued, all people were bundles of different traits; there were many selves in what Doyle, in a poem of the same title, called "The Inner Room" of his personality. An astute detective must have constituted one "strand" of his identity in order for him to have made Sherlock Holmes credible, but he could only have been a Holmes in real life by suppressing all his other selves. Holmes was, after all, a fiction, a character whose traits were exaggerated for artistic effect. Doyle playfully replied to "an undiscerning critic" who had accused him of ingratitude for having Holmes dismiss Poe's detective Dupin as inferior, despite Doyle's obvious debts to Poe, "Please grip this fact with your cerebral tentacle,/The doll and his maker are never identical."[7] Students of literature can benefit most from using biographical detail as the means to an end: greater insight into the processes by which fact is transformed into fiction.

Until relatively recently, the very popularity of the Holmes stories have presented something of an embarrassment to the literary critic; as the English writer Somerset Maugham confessed of Doyle, "he was greatly admired by the intelligentsia. . . they couldn't help enjoying his stories, but felt that it was hardly literature" (quoted in Nordon, 233)—that is, hardly "serious" literature—a prejudice that Doyle of course shared. Yet, of all the possible varieties of escapist popular literature, detective fiction offers the most obvious satisfactions to intellectuals, who can hardly see themselves as the typical romance or adventure hero but find ready and gratifying identification with the brilliant sleuth who masters the world through his powers of deduction.[8] The poets T. S. Eliot and W. H. Auden confessed themselves fans of the Holmes stories, and even Edmund Wilson, who earned the wrath of many devotees of detective fiction by denouncing the most popular of Doyle's successors as "sub-literary," allowed that "Sherlock Holmes *is* literature on a humble but not ignoble level."[9] The enthusiasm of such readers has helped at least in part to make detective fiction a more respectable subject of study; so, too, perhaps did the genteel settings and characters featured in the novels of the 1920s and 1930s, the so-called golden age of detective fiction in England. Sherlock Holmes has formed a cornerstone for most histories of the detective novel, as the model for the sort of eccentric gentleman detective who inspired Agatha Christie's Hercule Poirot, Dorothy Sayers's Lord Peter Wimsey, and a host of other golden-age sleuths.[10]

As literary critics have become more open to the cultural insights afforded by popular literature, detective fiction in general and the Holmes stories in particular have attracted attention from a variety of critical perspectives. Geraldine Pederson-Krag offered the classic Freudian paradigm for the detective story in 1949. She likened the unveiling of mystery in the detective tale to the child's witnessing for the first time the "primal scene" of his or her parents having sexual intercourse. Reading detective fiction, she hypothesized, helps one cope with the unresolved oedipal anxiety, jealousy, and guilt activated by such an experience: "The reader's ego need fear no punishment for libidinal or aggressive urges. In an orgy of investigation, the ego, personified by the great detective, can look, remember, and correlate without fear and without reproach in utter contrast to the ego of the terrified infant witnessing the primal scene." The sleuth's eccentricity and amateur status allow the reader to participate vicariously in his investigation while disavowing any personal identification or official responsibility. According to Pederson-Krag, the Dr. Watson character supplies a second line of defense: "Should the punishing superego threaten, the reader can point to this character and say, 'This is I. I was simply standing by.'"[11]

Pederson-Krag linked the appeal of detective fiction to what she claimed are universal psychological patterns shared by all readers; other critics have studied evidence from the Holmes stories more specifically for a revelation of the particular neuroses and preoccupations of Sir Arthur Conan Doyle. The results have been mixed: Samuel Rosenberg's loose grasp of the facts of Doyle's life and his heavy dependence on free association prevent his *Naked Is the Best Disguise* from making a very convincing case about Doyle's allusions to mythic patterns and his obsession with violence, sexual deviance, and punishment.[12] Christopher Redmond's *In Bed with Sherlock Holmes* more successfully uses the sexual subtexts of the Sherlock Holmes stories to suggest insights into the emotional dynamics of Doyle and other Victorians.[13] Still other critics have approached psychological issues historically, reading the Sherlock Holmes stories as a reflection of the mind of the times, which believed in, but needed reassurance about, the powers of scientific rationality to solve mysteries and maintain order.[14]

More recent theoretical approaches have also found fertile ground in the kind of popular literature that the Holmes stories represent. The formulaic nature of detective fiction has made it particularly useful to structuralist analyses that demonstrate the operation of more abstract patterns of action, theme, and character in literary works; the same traits have attracted the interest of narratologists who have used the detective story as a paradigm for understanding the ways story, plot, and meaning interact in most realist fiction. Semiotic studies have attempted to systematize the literary and philosophical implications of Holmesian patterns of deduction and interpretation of clues as signs of larger patterns of meaning.[15]

Detective fiction in general and Sherlock Holmes in particular have also figured prominently in recent theories about the ways in which literature shapes and communicates ideological values. Doyle's stories offer significant evidence of the nineteenth-century shift of attitudes on crime and social order: from criminal to detective, from punishment to detection, from imposing order by threat of violence to embodying order through conformity.[16] It is yet another tribute to the vitality of the Sherlock Holmes stories that they have attracted such diverse and committed critical attention. The chapters to come will examine the insights of these approaches and explore the ways in which they can enrich our reading of the Holmes canon.

A READING

4

Guilty Pleasures: Reading Detective Fiction

The rhetorical shape that any fiction takes—the characteristic ways in which it informs and convinces—can reveal much about the assumptions that it expects its readers to make concerning knowledge and reality. An analysis of the narrative structures of detective stories can help us be more knowing readers of a wide range of fiction. The development of their characteristic forms can also help us understand the historical relationship of popular to high art and the relationship of the detective genre to the larger dynamics of literary realism.

Appearing just as the tide of realist fiction was about to turn in the experimental directions of the twentieth century, the Holmes stories offered an exaggeration of realism's traits that throws its rhetorical strategies into higher relief. Their presentation as events that had really occurred and that could be independently corroborated by the reader made literal realism's claims to mirror life; their celebration of the power of facts and reason and their forceful drive toward closures that solved life's mysteries underscored realism's assumption that self and society were ordered in ways that made them ultimately transparent to the careful observer. Even now, the stylized patterns reiterated in their plotting make us aware of—and suspicious of—realism's attempts to erase the boundary between the natural and the contrived. The conventions of realism are so familiar to us that we are not always fully aware of the artificiality of those special properties and narrative practices that make this kind of writing an artistic text, a literary artifact. The textuality of realist fiction tends to become invisible to us as readers; its sequencing and selectivity seem natural: this is simply the way stories are told, we assume. Because of its more distinctive form and more limited objectives, detective fiction is more easily recognizable as a specific and formally demarcated genre. In actuality, though, its characteristic interactions between story and plot and its ways of controlling us as readers offer a paradigm for the textual dynamics of much realist fiction and can provide valuable insights into the psychological ends they serve.

Detective stories offer a classic example of what Roland Barthes called the "hermeneutic" text, the text motivated by the desire for an answer or solution to an enigma.[1] Such stories are governed by a paradoxical textual dynamics: they move toward solution but exist only so long as closure can be postponed. Our reading pleasure is intimately tied to the suspense that this postponement creates. In many literary works, the suspense inheres in whether and how the characters will find fulfillment of their desires. Elements of mystery may intervene, but they usually function as means to the end of the characters' self-realization. We are eager to learn the protagonist's true parentage in Sophocles' *Oedipus Rex* or his real benefactor in Dickens's *Great Expectations*, for instance, but these works' emotional emphasis is on how Oedipus and Pip respond morally to this information. Although detective plots often rely on Aristotelian elements like reversal, recognition, and suffering, these are seldom the means to significant change in the characters, particularly not in the main character, the detective. For detective fiction in the Doyle tradition, the solution to the mystery is an end in itself, and the solver seldom involves himself emotionally in crime or detection.[2]

As Dennis Porter pointed out, the success of the Holmes stories owes much to Doyle's skill in creating suspense by delaying the answers to the questions raised by the detective tale (Porter, 28). In the typical Holmes adventure, the enigma or mystery is formally posed early in the story, usually by the prospective client: a missing spouse, fiancé, or possession, an inexplicable sequence of events, an anticipated crime. Allowing the clients to tell their own stories keeps the reader outside the crime, sharing the clients' confusion and excluded from all of Holmes's insights, except those he deigns to reveal. The reader is baffled by bizarre and seemingly uninterpretable details—the strange demands of "The Red-Headed League" or of Violet Hunter's employer at the Copper Beeches—or is misled by false accusations of guilt, often against a sympathetic character: apparently, James McCarthy has murdered his father in Boscombe Valley, Arthur Holder has attempted to steal the Beryl Coronet to cover his gambling debts, a gypsy "band" is involved in the death of Julia Stoner. These false leads are sometimes reinforced by the endorsement of an official figure like Lestrade (BOSC, 1:275) or Bradstreet (ENGR, 1:385) of Scotland Yard, the headquarters of the London Metropolitan Police Force. We are further tantalized by Holmes's odd and enigmatic behavior, like his visit to Jabez Wilson's pawnshop or his elaborate charade outside Irene Adler's villa. Even after Holmes has dramatically confronted the wrongdoer with the truth and forced him to confess, our suspense does not end until he explains to Watson how he reached his conclusions.

The narrative interaction between Holmes and Watson is crucial to our enjoyment of delay. Once the mystery has been devised, the author's main problem is one of concealment: how to limit the revelation of the solution long enough to maintain the reader's interest. Although authors using third-person narrators can accomplish this by limiting their omniscience, there is always a certain amount of conscious concealment of important information on the author's part that may try the reader's patience. Alternatively, making the detective a first-person narrator would provide the author a more straightforward excuse for limiting the narrator's knowledge, but would also make it more difficult to obtain the dramatic effects that the sudden and unanticipated solution of the crime provides. We would hardly tolerate the withholding of crucial information by a first-person narrator, but it is more difficult to manage suspense without it.[3] The magician's tricks would also lose some of their glamour if they were narrated while being performed. In two early stories for the most part told by Holmes to Watson ("The Gloria Scott" and "The Musgrave Ritual"), the cases unfold in such a way as to lose little suspense by being re-created by Holmes as he experienced them; the full explanation of the first one becomes complete only with the reading of the dead man's private papers at the end of the story, for instance. The late stories that Holmes narrates directly, "The Blanched Soldier" and "The Lion's Mane," maintain suspense only by virtue of an elaborately misleading set of false clues and Holmes's annoying refusal to explain the correct interpretation for several pages after he has obviously determined it.

Doyle usually solved these narrative problems in the same way that Poe had: by using a first-person narrator who is not the detective to chronicle his feats. Doyle planned Watson as "commonplace" foil and comrade to Holmes (M&A, 69), someone who could give a first-hand description of the adventures he had participated in but who was sufficiently excluded from Holmes's thoughts to maintain the suspense. Even his eyewitness authority is in a sense artificial: since Watson narrates all Holmes's cases after the fact, in the telling he must suppress his knowledge of how they turned out in order to re-create the puzzlement and surprise he felt at the time. Watson is a stand-in for the reader to the extent that we share the limits of what he knows and when. But his limitations are also calculated to make the reader feel superior. As Doyle put it, all hint of wit or wisdom "is remorselessly eliminated so that he may be Watson."[4] He is the perfect straight man. No matter how many times he is witness to Holmes's reasoning abilities, he never quite learns how to duplicate them. He can manage to record every detail of Mary Sutherland's dress while still "miss[ing] everything of importance" that indicates her personality and recent behavior (IDEN, 1:260). He is fussily self-conscious of his importance as narrator, slightly snobbish about the vulgar richness of the King of Bohemia's dress (SCAN, 1:213) or of Mary Sutherland's finery (IDEN, 1:260), primly disapproving of Holmes's excesses (his cocaine use and his egotism, for example). Stephen Knight aptly assigned his tone to "the voice of a mildly self-satisfied bourgeois who feels he has a mastery of things"; our very suspicions that he is inade-

quate to the problems he faces help ally us more closely with Holmes
in a desire to share in his real mastery of the situation (Knight, 84–85).
Of course, we cannot entirely blame Watson's failures of understanding on his slow wit, for Doyle quite deliberately withholds information by obscuring the meaning of Holmes's actions at key stages of
the investigation. We marvel with Watson at his disguises, but are seldom allowed to see him in action while wearing them. Even when we
witness his masquerade as a "simple-minded Nonconformist clergyman" in "A Scandal in Bohemia" (1:222), its exact motives are not
explained until after the fact. His even more dramatic impersonation
of an opium addict in "The Man with the Twisted Lip" is only tangen-
tially connected to the story's central mystery. More often, Holmes
simply vanishes for several hours (whether disguised or not), leaving
Watson alone to "cudgel his brains" over the case's "mysteries and
improbabilities," to suggest misleading solutions, and to intensify our
awe at the brilliance that will, he reassures us, lead Holmes to triumph
in the end (BOSC, 1:277–78). Or he just as enigmatically withdraws
into a "three-pipe" meditation (REDH, 1:241) while Watson dozes, to
emerge minutes or hours later with his mind made up (TWIS, 1:321).
The dramatic conclusions to the stories usually depend upon his suppressing what he has learned or decided until after the solution has
been revealed, often by the wrongdoers themselves, who have been
maneuvered by Holmes into confrontation and confession. Only then
does he finally reconstruct for Watson the chains of reasoning that led
him to his final conclusions. Watson may tell the story, in other words,
but Doyle allows Holmes to control the knowledge that is power in
the world of detection.

This disjunction between what has happened and what we are
told suggests another way in which detective fiction throws into
greater relief textual dynamics that it shares with other kinds of narrative. Russian formalist critics have used the terms *fabula* and *sjužet*,
respectively, to distinguish between the order of the events referred to
in a fiction (what happened) and the order in which these events are
presented in narrative (how the story is told). Foreshadowings, flash-
backs, and omissions of information in the *sjužet*, or "plot," as it is usually translated, can make it different from the *fabula*, or story; plot

provides an interpretation of the events that constitute the story.[5] For Tzvetan Todorov, detective fictions offer a paradigmatic example of the way plots relate to stories. Such works in effect contain two narratives, that of the crime and that of its investigation. Todorov considered these narratives roughly equivalent to *fabula* and *sjužet*, respectively, noting that the purpose of the investigation, or *sjužet*, is to re-create the crime, the original story that, while it must remain absent from the narrative until the very end, has actually brought the detective tale into being. In a sense, then, the crime is the "story" that motivates both narratives (Todorov, 44–46). In *Reading for the Plot*, Peter Brooks used the Sherlock Holmes adventure "The Musgrave Ritual" as a particularly literal example of how the detection reconstructs the crime. To solve this mystery, Holmes precisely duplicates the criminal's behavior, following the same coded set of instructions that the wrongdoer used, until he is led to his body. Similar if less thorough examples can be found in Holmes's trademark combing of the crime scene in Boscombe Valley for clues that allow him to describe the murderer's clothing and appearance or his tracing back of the goose that concealed the Blue Carbuncle. As Glenn Most put it, the detective's investigations attempt to duplicate the wrongdoers' actions or thoughts in order to formulate a mental version of the crime that can then be tested and revised until it is brought into correspondence with the actual deed.[6]

The gradual coalescence of investigation with crime was a technique Doyle mastered over time. *A Study in Scarlet* breaks into two separate narratives: Holmes's capture of Enoch Drebber's murderer at the end of the first part leaves both method and motive unexplained. It requires a second narrative, supplied in part by an omniscient narrator, in part by Jefferson Hope, to reconstruct the previous crimes in America leading up to Hope's revenge upon Drebber. Only then does Holmes finish the story by explaining the process of "reasoning backward" that has allowed him to track Hope down (STUD, 1:99–100). *The Sign of Four* also depends upon a double plotted structure, the first the revelation of how Bartholomew Sholto's death was effected in England and the second narrative by Jonathan Small, explaining the exotic mixture of stolen treasure and betrayed loyalties that motivated the murder. Shifting to short stories helped Doyle by providing a briefer span of narrative over which the complete solution had to be concealed, but in them he also tended to rely on more domesticated crimes that required less exotic, and hence more easily explained, motives. He was thus able more easily to integrate the how with the why of the crime. Works like "Boscombe Valley" or "Noble Bachelor" still rely on the introduction of a foreign plot late in the story to explain the reasons for the deeds that occur, but more often readers already possess most of the relevant evidence and have been supplied with plausible but misleading motives, even if we still need Holmes to explain how to interpret these correctly at the end of the story.

For Brooks, the detective's retracing of the criminal's steps literalizes the "interpretive ordering" of *fabula* by *sjužet* that most narratives claim to accomplish, insofar as they present themselves as repeating something that has already happened. Detective fiction also dramatizes the implicit contradictions that result from the fact that prior events or causes can only be realized to be such in retrospect; although events are presumed to precede and to justify the narratives constructed about them, many narratives give the impression of creating events to justify the results they need in order to make sense. This is particularly clear in the detective story, which uses "the plot of the inquest to find, or construct, a story of the crime which will offer just those features necessary to the thematic coherence we call a solution, while claiming, of course, that the solution has been made necessary by the crime" (Brooks, 29). Holmes's genius is largely a question of his ability to identify and interpret correctly those details that actually constitute the narrative of the crime: to realize that the bizarre requirements of the Red-Headed League are simply a diversion from the real action of the bank robbery, for instance, or that the remnants of the hotel bill on the back of the note constitute the real clue in "Noble Bachelor." Brooks set the detective story's pervasive concern with causal links in a historical context by seeing it as part of a larger nineteenth-century preoccupation with producing life histories that could replace the religious texts that offered earlier ages "a sacred masterplot that organizes and explains the world" (Brooks, 6). This preoccupation may be most evident in those bildungsromans, or "novels of development," that, like *Great Expectations* or *Jane Eyre*, reconstruct the past to explain and to justify the protagonist's present position, but it is also evident in the much more widely held assumption in nineteenth-century fiction that the way to understand individuals and social groups is by following portions of their histories. Becoming most popular in an era when social harmony and the unity of the individual personality seemed increasingly problematic and threatened by disintegration, detective fiction, like the Freudian psychoanalysis that developed contemporaneously with it, reassures readers that from the fragmentary and confusing evidence left in the present, a coherent, logically causal narrative of the past can still be constructed to give meaning to even the most bizarre events (Brooks, 269–70).

Given its intensification or concentration of effects shared with a broad mainstream of nineteenth-century realism, the detective story has attracted negative criticism from theorists who value narratives that resist and problematize, rather than gratify, the reader's desire for meaning and order. For the detective story in the Doyle tradition, as opposed to the "hard-boiled" American genre that developed in the 1920s and 1930s, the possibility of finding a correct solution is never in doubt, even though the criminals may sometimes escape (as in "The Engineer's Thumb" or "The Five Orange Pips"). Because the detective ultimately gains total mastery over the process of interpretation, for Glenn Most he figuratively represents the ideal reader. The methods the detective applies to the crime closely duplicate those the reader applies to the story of the investigation: both are striving to find the correct reading of the evidence. Watson represents the wrong kinds of interpretive processes that readers must exert themselves to avoid, while the Holmes character "represents the ideal pole of perfect knowledge, of an entirely correct reading, towards which the reader aims and which he ought never quite be able to attain" (Most, 349) if the detective is to maintain his appeal and the story an adequate amount of suspense.

But it is precisely this model of reading that has been challenged by recent literary theories that stress the instability of the reasoning process and question the ability of language to control meaning. From this perspective, the Holmesian detective story can only reassure readers of the complete interpretability of reality by suppressing what is ambiguous and denying what is psychologically uncontrollable. The nineteenth-century way of telling a story was the counterpart of its confidence in the unity of the self and the power of rationality. It was these assumptions that early twentieth-century writers like Virginia Woolf or James Joyce challenged by fragmenting point of view, disrupting chronology, and denying plots complete closure. During this same period, the English detective novel continued to offer the reader a familiar experience of narrative mastery that in effect evaded the philosophical challenges mounted by modernism. Indeed, at the very time when modernist texts were rejecting the rules of nineteenth-century realism, writers of detective fiction were formalizing stricter rules for their own genre.[7] The continued popularity of the Holmes stories in the early modern period owed something to the reassurances they offered about both the reading process and ways of knowing the world at a time when other fictions had begun purposefully to withhold these.[8]

For other critics, the demands the detective story makes on character and plot render it "radically antinovelistic,"[9] even by nineteenth-century standards. As Doyle himself freely acknowledged, Holmes was purposefully oversimplified to maintain the focus on the plot: "His character admits of no light or shade. He is a calculating machine, and anything you add to that simply weakens the effect" (M&A, 103). The various evidences of his eccentricities reiterate, rather than complicate, his personality, so that there is no real character development. According to Michael Holquist, Sherlock Holmes "does not really *exist* when he is not on a case.... He *is* his function." For Holquist, plot is as static as character in the Holmes stories. Because Holmes is more a puzzle breaker than a crime solver, there is a sense that "*nothing* really happens" in these tales. Or as Todorov put it, once the criminal activity has taken place, the characters in the detective story learn rather than act.[10] "The Five Orange Pips," which takes place almost entirely in Holmes and Watson's Baker Street rooms, is an extreme example, of course, but we must admit that notwithstanding the dramatic moments provided by Holmes's capture of the bank robbers in "The Red-Headed League" or his attack on the swamp adder in "The Speckled Band," for instance, his "adventures" are usually more mental than physical, made up largely of conversations about deeds rather than deeds themselves: long descriptions by clients that set up the mysteries and Holmes's closing remarks on how he figured it out. Perhaps we get as much enjoyment from the ingenuity of the problem as from its solution, just as those throw-away deductions that have nothing to do with solving the mystery (like Holmes's discovery that Watson has a careless housemaid [SCAN, 1:211] or that his bedroom window is on the right side of the room [BOSC, 1:271]) are often more entertaining than the exercise of reasoning that eventually solves the crime. Martin Kayman, who stressed the differences between the Holmesian detective who tried to close off mystery and his forerunners (such as Poe's Dupin) who acknowledged its powers, argued that Watson's repeated allusions to other cases that we as readers are supposed to have read about in the papers and whose factuality we are not allowed to doubt reinforce the type of narrative mastery the stories assert by "obliging us to believe only in the text's testimony of what we are not allowed to know." The authority of Holmesian detective narrative is in this sense based on "the deliberate repression of the very category" of the fictional.[11]

We may acknowledge the strength of all of these criticisms but still not be willing to surrender the undeniable pleasure the Sherlock Holmes stories bring us. A more fruitful way of understanding this pleasure and its relationship to our assumptions and desires about reality may be to assess the Holmes adventures by the rather different aesthetic objectives of popular literature, rather than to focus on their failure to rival the challenges of high art. The following chapter examines this aesthetic and the social and artistic background out of which Sherlock Holmes developed and considers the desires that detective literature has traditionally gratified.

5

Sherlock Holmes and the Formulas of Detection

"Who Cares Who Killed Roger Ackroyd?" Edmund Wilson indignantly asked in a 1945 attack on detective fiction as "sub-literary." Responding in part to the popularity of works like Agatha Christie's *The Murder of Roger Ackroyd*, Wilson here sounded the keynote for a long debate about the value of such stories, a debate calculated to make those who enjoy mysteries feel somewhat apologetic, if not actually guilty, about their tastes. The debate has as much to do with the position of popular literature in modern culture as it does with the merits of the genre per se, and the very fact that an intellectual like Wilson went out of his way to attack detective fiction offers suggestive evidence about the pressure that popular culture had begun to exert on the debate about what constitutes art.

Increasing acknowledgment of the power of popular literature in recent years has helped decenter the debate about defining "great" art by shifting the focus away from what we should like to the reasons for, and effects of, our enjoyment of those forms that we do enjoy. The following discussion examines the changing assumptions about detection and social order that shaped the development of crime fiction as a genre and positions Sherlock Holmes in this wider literary and social context.

THE AESTHETICS OF POPULAR LITERATURE

Tzvetan Todorov helped us isolate the differences between high and popular art forms by pointing out that the former values originality much more highly. With high art, we assume that it is a sign of inferiority for a work to resemble a conventional model too closely. Where the high-art masterpiece is precisely the work that can define its own conventions, popular literature is deemed successful by how well it satisfies the conventions of its particular genre. Try to improve too much on detective fiction, and one ends up writing "literature" instead (Todorov, 43). Readers are attracted to detective stories, just as they are attracted to science fiction or Gothic romances, because they know these will satisfy certain formal expectations about plot, character, and emotion. Their familiarity with the genre's literary formulas helps guide their understanding and appreciation of new works. The success of what John Cawelti called "formula stories" depends upon a balance of innovation and conformity; the work must offer details sufficiently distinctive to satisfy the reader's desire for novelty, but these innovations "must ultimately work toward the fulfillment of the conventional form" in order to satisfy the reader's expectations about genre.[1]

Still, the author's ability to create artful variations in the formula is crucially important precisely because there is so much else about the form that is standardized. The Sherlock Holmes stories offer interesting perspectives on such variations on a theme. Their very success helped give detection the status of a formula by endowing the brilliant, eccentric amateur suggested by Poe with a vehicle that could appeal to the popular imagination. As I suggested earlier, this appeal rests in part on Doyle's ability to evoke an imaginary world that offers the pleasures of recognizable landmarks and the escape of nostalgia. Both Cawelti and Porter noted that the reassurance that formula fiction offers readers owes much to stereotypes of class, ethnicity, and landscape, fixed cultural entities that reinforce the security of a shared fantasy. Porter characterized Doyle's London as "mythic" in the sense that it relies on a kind of metonymic shorthand to suggest the feeling of place with a few strategic and characteristically British details; the most successful detective writers, he argued, are, like Doyle, "the distillers of familiar national essences" that possess all the romantic charm and none of the banality of the real thing (Porter, 217–18; Cawelti, 19, 31–35). Still other critics have likened the Holmesian detective story to the comedy of manners, insofar as both depend upon witty variations on recognizable conventions and social types, punish social deviants, and highlight the sophisticated brilliance of a well-bred hero.[2]

It is the character of Holmes that offers the most interesting possibilities for the interplay between stereotype and variation, or, as Martin Priestman (91) called it, reproducibility and singularity. Holmes's genteel eccentricity, cool urbanity, and dramatic deductions refreshed older detective stereotypes so distinctively as to create a new archetype. But once established as part of a type, his very uniqueness becomes in a sense typical. We turn to Holmes's stories in part to have our expectations about his eccentricities reinforced, just as we anticipate and take pleasure from further reiterations of the utterly predictable behavior of Dickens's eccentric characters.[3] We anticipate the displays of his encyclopedic knowledge as well as those startling deductions of a character's identity or behavior. We learn to expect his dreamy distraction when listening to clients and his avidity in scouring a crime scene for clues, his disguises, his disdain for the official police force, his boredom when not on a case. Precisely because Holmes is always so much the same, we relish all the more those minor details that vary the pattern. He is prevented from being a complete "reasoning and observing machine" (SCAN, 1:209) by his artistic affinities with music (REDH, 1:243) and his escapist dabbling in drugs (SCAN, 1:209), as well as by his surprising display of physical strength, as when he straightens the poker bent by Dr. Grimesby Roylott in "The Speckled Band" (1:357). As Doyle (reluctantly) expanded the Holmes saga into new series of short stories after the *Adventures*, he perhaps thought it necessary to include additional glimpses of Holmes's personality and background to maintain audience interest. At the beginning of "The Musgrave Ritual," for instance, we find his bohemianism elaborated by such extravagant behavior as storing his tobacco in a slipper and using his sitting room wall for target practice (1:527–28). A glimpse of his college days in "Gloria Scott" (1:511) and the revelation that he has an older brother, Mycroft, in "The Greek Interpreter" help prevent him from seeming completely "inhuman" to Watson (GREE, 1:595), as does his brief display of genuine concern when Watson is wounded in "The Three Garridebs" (2:562). Priestman found it somewhat ironic that Holmes, who professes himself a connoisseur of the bizarre and the unusual and who turns to cocaine to dull the tedium of a world without sufficiently interesting problems, is himself "routine incarnate" when it comes to the ways in which he solves crimes. As he pointed out, however, the success of a series depends upon just such endless repetition or reproducibility. The main characters cannot develop too far without heading for some kind of closure that would terminate the series; they thus wind up suspended in a nondirectional sameness, an effect aided in the Holmes saga by the relative lack of correspondence between the order in which the adventures purportedly took place and the order in which Watson chronicles them (Priestman, 93–94).

For Doyle's contemporaries, however, it was surely Holmes's perceived improvements on earlier models of the detective that earned their loyalty as readers. To understand the significance of the innovations he offered, we need to examine the literary tradition out of which he emerged. As Cawelti argued, particular literary formulas become popular at particular times because of their success in developing artistic conventions that represent and relate a wide, and widely held, variety of values, symbols, and themes. Story patterns persist by virtue of their continued ability to give satisfying artistic unity to a range of ideological and psychological preoccupations in later eras (Cawelti, 20, 30). The rise of the detective tradition traces important shifts in the Western world's attitudes toward crime, individuality, and social order during the nineteenth century.

INVENTING THE DETECTIVE

Detective fiction is as much a cultural as a literary phenomenon. The emergence of the detective as a type registers shifts in the cultural consensus on what constituted crime and its appropriate punishment. Eighteenth-century Europe tended to thematize social conflict in terms of an opposition between nature and an unreasonable social order. The severity of criminal codes and the barbarity of public executions and other corporal punishment encouraged a general hostility against the law as a victimizer of the powerless many by the powerful few. Such perceptions were reinforced by British laws like the Riot Act of 1715, which criminalized the political expression of the disenfranchised and in effect declared parliamentary government the only legitimate form of political behavior (Kayman, 37). From such a perspective, the bandit could be heroized for his legitimate defiance of unjust authority, and the officials who opposed him were reviled as thief-takers and informers, bounty hunters in service to aristocratic oppressors. As the middle classes began to gain in wealth and power during the early decades of the nineteenth century and gained more of a stake in the maintenance of public order, however, whatever populist sympathies they may have had with the bandit began to shift. The reform of legal codes and the replacement of the gallows by the prison as the main instrument of punishment allowed them to view the law more favorably, while the economic instabilities attendant upon industrialization led them increasingly to identify the impoverished and potentially revolutionary masses, rather than the aristocracy, as the greatest threat to their interests and security. Thus, the bandit was gradually transformed from a rebel to a criminal, and the police, from a potentially intrusive and wasteful instrument of state power to a force necessary to ensure legitimate order.[4]

We can find literary manifestations of this transformation in the shift of interest from criminal to detective and from crime to investigation in popular fiction. The criminal protagonists of early eighteenth-century works like Daniel Defoe's *Moll Flanders* (1722) or Henry Fielding's *Jonathan Wild* (1743), although dutifully punished, earn the reader's grudging admiration and sympathy in chronicles that detail their crimes at length. Evidence of a continuing public fascination with criminal wrongdoing can be found in the less artistically distinguished *Newgate Calendar,* a compilation of stories about notorious crimes and their punishments. Named after the famous London criminal prison, the first series of *Newgate Calendar* stories was published in 1773, with updated versions appearing periodically from 1809 through the rest of nineteenth century. In the "Newgate novels" of the 1830s and 1840s, authors like William Harrison Ainsworth and Edward Bulwer-Lytton catered to the same public appetites for criminality with romanticized tales of dashing highwaymen and famous thieves. But subtle differences in intention and reception were already becoming evident. Bulwer-Lytton struck a reformist note in his *Paul Clifford* (1830), which echoed contemporary criticism of the injustice of the penal code. This did not save him from being attacked for romanticizing crime in his next Newgate novel, *Eugene Aram* (1832). One of his chief attackers, William Makepeace Thackeray, represented the emerging attitude in his novel *Catherine* (1839–40), an ironic debunking of the tendency to idealize the criminal world.[5]

The stage was thus set for the appearance of new works in which the criminal investigator, not the criminal, was the main focus. Stephen Knight argued that the *Newgate Calendar* stories tended to treat crime as a natural outgrowth of the criminal's betrayal of familial and social duties and to assume that capture was inevitable. The wrongdoer is betrayed into recklessness and eventually into penitence by his guilty conscience or captured so quickly and easily as to suggest that escape is never a real possibility. The implication is that no special agent of detection and enforcement is necessary in a society in which ideological and religious consensus acts as a collective protection against successful challenges to social order. But this consensus was already breaking down at the time, suggesting that such tales functioned more as wishful thinking than as confident assertion. Once the criminal was "no longer seen as an aberrant member of society but as a member of a hostile class," the detective's specialized skills were needed to combat crime both historically and fictionally (Knight 11–13, 34).

Sherlock Holmes and the Formulas of Detection

A transitional figure in this process was François Eugène Vidocq (1775–1857), a thief turned thief-taker who became a secret agent for the Paris police and later founded the first known private detective agency. His dramatic successes in entrapping criminals (artistically heightened by ghostwriters) were first chronicled in his 1828 *Memoirs of Vidocq*. He established a number of devices that would become conventional among later detectives: a contempt for the official police as hopeless bunglers, at least when compared to the brilliant special agent; a histrionic penchant for disguise and surprise entrapments of wrongdoers; and an extensive knowledge of the criminal underworld. Vidocq's popularity inspired French novelists like Honoré de Balzac, Eugène Sue, and Alexandre Dumas *père* to feature detective figures and methods in numerous serialized novels in the 1840s and 1850s. The detective really came into his own in the *romans policiers* (literally, "police novels") of the 1850s and 1860s, the most famous of which were written by Émile Gaboriau. Gaboriau's stylish police detective Monsieur Lecoq joined brilliant reasoning abilities with scientific methods of tracking and identifying criminals and a flair for dramatic solutions. Less showy British versions of this type during the same era included supporting characters like Inspector Bucket in Charles Dickens's *Bleak House* (1852–53) and Sergeant Cuff in Wilkie Collins's *The Moonstone* (1868) (Murch, 42–46; 51–52; 121–27).

Most influential as a model for Sherlock Holmes and British golden-age detectives was not the professional agent of the police but the eccentric amateur, epitomized by Edgar Allan Poe's Monsieur C. Auguste Dupin, who was first featured in the 1841 short story "The Murders in the Rue Morgue" and again in "The Mystery of Marie Rogêt" (1842) and "The Purloined Letter" (1844). The rivalry between Dupin and the prefect of police, who grudgingly asks his assistance, owes something to Vidocq's example, but Poe also has Dupin criticize Vidocq for relying on guesses rather than "educated thought" to solve mysteries. The son of an "illustrious" but impoverished family, Dupin commands a range of culture and learning out of Vidocq's reach and uses it brilliantly to inform his investigations of material clues and the feats of reasoning and deduction based on them. Reinforced by his lectures on the methodology of detection, Dupin's adventures encouraged the shift of interest from crime to detection evident in the transition from the serialized crime novels of the 1840s and 1850s to the *romans policiers* of the following decades (Murch, 72).

Class identification was important to the fictional evolution of the detective. Vidocq's power comes in part from his having been part of the criminal underworld; indeed, the first volume and a half of his four-volume memoirs deal with his adventures on the other side of the law, and we get more information about crime than about detection in his stories. He is essentially a spy who succeeds largely because of his personal knowledge of the language, habits, and tricks that were presumed to set the criminal class apart. In an era when the French public would still have viewed this kind of police agent with ambivalence, Sue's *Mystères de Paris* (Mysteries of Paris, 1842–43) and Dumas's *Le Comte de Monte-Cristo* (The Count of Monte Cristo, 1845–46) instead feature aristocratic heroes whose ability to solve mysteries is more an avocation than a profession. Dumas's *Les Mohicans de Paris* (The Mohicans of Paris, 1854–55) divides the detective function between the aristocratic amateur Salvator and the police officer Jackal, who, while sympathetically portrayed, is unequivocally positioned as Salvator's social inferior. Upon his introduction as a minor character, Gaboriau's Lecoq is presented as a former lawbreaker turned policeman, not unlike Vidocq. When Gaboriau promoted him to hero of later novels (beginning with *Monsieur Lecoq* in 1869), however, he took care to give him a respectable family background and a university education and to suggest that his only involvement in crime was to have planned perfect ones in his imagination. Lecoq's intelligence, his varied skills, and the glimpses he offered into the intricacies of police work did much to give the police detective a more favorable image in the public eye. In England, Dickens worked to accomplish this same end with Inspector Bucket, who, despite his at best lower-middle-class status, possesses a quiet professional competence that proves crucial to revealing—and presumably helping to right—the failings of a decaying gentry.[6]

Ultimately, however, glamorizing the abilities of the working-class or lower-middle-class policeman would do little to advance middle-class claims for their own social prestige, and by the end of the nineteenth century the most distinguished British example of the detective had become the unequivocally genteel amateur—the Dupin rather than the Bucket (Mandel, 14–15). Holmes, it is true, draws widely on both types of detective. He possesses Vidocq's expertise about criminal life and Lecoq's scientific techniques for identifying and interpreting clues. Although sharing Dupin's abstract powers of reason, he is more actively involved in the pursuit of crime than that armchair genius, and his social roots are in the country gentry rather than in the illustrious nobility. The real appeal of his character lies in its ability to satisfy a middle-class ideal of preeminence earned by talent rather than by birth while still retaining the trappings of older, leisured aristocratic ideals. Porter and others have noted how the roles of the gentleman and the amateur reinforce each other in Holmes's characterization. The gentleman detective could afford to be disinterested, to serve as a "higher public servant" for the sake of sheer intellectual challenge, unmotivated by salary and under no obligation to prove himself to an employer. Amateur detection was more like the virtuoso display of the artist than the work of the bureaucratic functionary; no wonder the would-be sleuth in Robert Louis Stevenson's *The Dynamiter* assures his friend that detection was "the only profession for a gentleman."[7] Holmes's celibacy, his emotional isolation, and his artistic proclivities distance him still further from the ordinary professional worker. The fashionable eccentricity of his cultured bachelor life and the effortless grace of his detections were symbolically the natural prerogative of the man of leisure. Thus, Holmes might share in the methods and the open-air adventures of the policeman, but only he possesses the class, education, and style to fulfill a cult of heroism still reserved to gentlemen (Porter, 155–57; Kayman, 215–16).

And unlike Inspector Bucket, who exposes the humiliating secrets of the gentry, the gentleman amateur can be trusted to protect the privacy of his middle- and upper-class clients. His natural province, in fact, is less the criminal world of the police detective than those polite or high circles of society where dishonor, betrayal, and scandal are the most serious dangers. His objective is more often the solution of mysteries than of crimes. In "The Purloined Letter," Dupin acts to protect the queen from blackmail, for instance. Although women have been killed in the rue Morgue, it is questionable whether an animal can be considered guilty of their "murder." And in five of the dozen *Adventures of Sherlock Holmes* (as well as in many later stories) no actual crime is committed. The detective, most often depicted in individualized combat with the criminal, has from his inception as a type worked to deflect examination of the legitimacy of law or consideration of the social and historical roots of crime by turning detection into a standoff between good and evil. The pure intellectuality of a Dupin distances inquiry even further, encouraging the belief that the puzzle-solving abilities of the isolated intellectual are adequate to defeat society's problems.[8] In combining the skills of both types of detective, Holmes exploits the silence of each about the ideological significance of crime.

The evolution of Sherlock Holmes as a character suggests a movement toward a more conservative social function over time. Just as the plots of the early novels, *A Study in Scarlet* and *The Sign of Four*, relied on the kind of exotic revenge motifs common to the sensational "shilling shockers" of the day, Holmes was in them also a more extreme type than he would become for the middle-class audience of the *Strand Magazine* stories. Holmes's use of cocaine to escape the tedium of the commonplace suggests the extravagant habits adopted by decadent artists to shock the middle-class public in the 1890s. His impersonal dedication to the science of detection parallels the attitudes of those who supported "art for art's sake": the speculation of Holmes's friend Stamford in *A Study in Scarlet* (1:6) that Holmes would give a person poison simply to note the results or the fact that he had beaten a cadaver to see how long after death bruises could form suggests that same intellectual curiosity for new knowledge and sensations, quite apart from moral considerations, endorsed by the aesthetes of the fin de siècle.[9] Although Holmes remains a character whose "life is spent in one long effort to escape from the commonplaces of existence" (REDH, 1:251), his resort to cocaine dwindles to mere allusions in the later stories. Notwithstanding the eccentric selectivity of his learning as outlined by Watson in *Study in Scarlet* (no knowledge of literature, philosophy, or astronomy, for instance; 1:12–13), the later Holmes is conversant with authors and thinkers familiar to the average cultured man of his time, carrying a "pocket Petrarch" and discussing George Meredith in "The Boscombe Valley Mystery" (1:275, 279).

As Doyle noted, the Holmes of *A Study in Scarlet* was "a mere calculating machine, but I had to make him more of an educated human being as I went on with him."[10] The reclusive scientist thus becomes a capable musician, composer, and concertgoer as well, equally at home with his "black-letter editions" of early books as with his test tubes (REDH, 1:243), and in later stories develops an even wider range of scholarly interests. Illustrator Sidney Paget's transformation of the gaunt, sharp-eyed, hawk-nosed Holmes of the early stories (STUD, 1:10) into the elegant gentleman of the *Adventures* was paralleled by the tempering of Holmes's pursuit of bizarre puzzles for their own sake with a more chivalrous concern to maintain social order and standards of decency and fair play. It is hardly coincidental that Holmes's growing conventionality corresponded with Doyle's growing security as a writer. The creator of *A Study in Scarlet* was a struggling doctor, with no guarantee of either artistic or professional success; his early Holmes was also an unestablished outsider, unable to afford comfortable rooms without Watson's partnership and happy to get a motley assortment of nondescript people as his clientele (STUD, 1:13). By the early 1890s, thanks largely to the success of the Sherlock Holmes stories, Doyle found his income and his reputation as a writer secure, indeed comfortable; little wonder that Holmes, too, famous enough in "A Scandal in Bohemia" to attract the patronage of royalty, also mellowed somewhat with regard to the habits and values of a status quo that had so graciously embraced his creator as one of its own.

The success of Sherlock Holmes inspired an entire generation of detective writers in England. Although R. Austin Freeman explored the scientific abilities of the detective, in his Dr. John Thorndyke, far more extensively than Doyle ever did, the more popular British type remained for decades the gentleman amateur who is guided more by a logical mind and an insight into human nature than by the specialized technologies of criminal investigation. We see him again in G. K. Chesterton's Father Brown and Edmund Clerihew Bentley's Philip Trent; he was brought to perfection in golden-age heroes of the 1920s and 1930s, notably Agatha Christie's Hercule Poirot and Dorothy Sayers's Lord Peter Wimsey. As the detective story expanded into the novel during this period, the detective had to acquire a somewhat fuller social dimension. But interest in these novels was also broadened to focus at least as much on the community disrupted by the crime as on the detective. These novelists paint a detailed canvas of social types and local color, often choosing the country house or other upper-class settings and peopling them with stock characters, of which the eccentric detective becomes simply one more. The villain of these stories is less likely to be a criminal than a member of society who has somehow violated the norms of his or her class or culture and must be punished by isolation and finally expulsion so that the society can remain stable (Mandel, 45; Grella, 40–44). In both social setting and the treatment of crime as self-contained, these stories express a nostalgia for an age and a stability already dissolving. It was left to American writers like Dashiell Hammett and Raymond Chandler to come to grips with the disintegrating effects of twentieth-century life. Their hard-boiled detectives exert far less mastery over the investigations in which they become personally involved and by which they often wind up damaged. Just as they operate in a much murkier atmosphere, where social behavior is far less predictable than in the English ideal, their styles of detection focus much more on the uncertainties of interpretation than on the assurance of results.

Considering the detective as a formulaic figure of popular literature who embodies important values and attitudes of a particular era need not exclude an appreciation of his relationship to more general literary archetypes; indeed, formulas can provide significant verification of the cultural importance of such archetypes. Several critics have noted the similarities between behavior and function of the Holmesian detective and those of the epic or folkloric hero, for instance. Folklore's purpose is largely normative: it is a means by which a culture defines and justifies its identity. By repeatedly presenting a hero confronting and vanquishing recognizable psychic and physical threats, the Holmes stories reassure readers about the essential correctness of their values and the security of their social order. Insofar as epics seek to accomplish similar ends, it is not surprising to find Holmes marked by many traits typical of the epic hero, Homer's Odysseus or the knights of the Grail legend, for instance. He is set apart from ordinary people by his extraordinary abilities, his knowledge, and his reason. He serves no superior; he undertakes his feats for the sake of his craft, as shows of pure virtuosity. He defines his own code of conduct rather than submitting to conventional moral or legal limits. Like the heroes of ancient epics, he appears in medias res, in the middle of things, and his exact origins are shadowy. In loosely connected episodes, his character is reiterated through trademarks of appearance and expression rather than being developed. Like the medieval knight, he operates in a celibate, essentially male world of action and challenge, although he is chivalrously devoted to righting wrongs against damsels in distress. He satisfies the most dramatic archetypal pattern of all by triumphing over death when he is resurrected after his final struggle with his archenemy Moriarty at the Reichenbach Falls (Knight, 103–4; Accardo, 17–18). W. H. Auden drew on this same Christian symbolism when he characterized the detective as "the exceptional individual who is in a state of grace" and who can thus absolve readers of their collective guilt and indulge their fantasies of "being restored to the Garden of Eden" (Auden, 21, 24).

Such heroic archetypes remain universal precisely because of their ability to change with time, however; if they speak to unchanging needs for reassurance and transcendence, they must also be available for updating to avoid being discarded as archaic and unrecognizable. Because of their simplicity, popular-fiction formulas allow the contours of archetypes to show through clearly. But, by virtue of their very popularity, these formulas also clothe those contours in specific forms that have widespread credibility for a given society. Thus, they are able to furnish invaluable insights into the way their readers organize reality and resolve or evade conflicts in their values. The shift from the infallible, impervious, stylish sleuth of the British tradition to the flawed vulnerability of the hard-boiled American private eye registers not just a change in styles but a change in worldview, with a sense of the greater fluidity of American culture and a growing anxiety about the difficulties of separating the guilty from the innocent. The very insistence with which our society obsessively turns out new versions of detective and police formulas suggests that we are still much in need of the kind of reassurance about our social order that these formulas have always promised to furnish. As we shall see in the following chapters, Sherlock Holmes's methods of investigation and deduction can tell us much about the scientific assumptions of the nineteenth century, but they also depend on reasoning strategies that remain essential to creating the order and mastery that we still crave.

6

"You Know My Methods"

Sherlock Holmes is of course most memorable for his dazzling feats of reasoning, those inferences that never fail to astonish Watson and his clients, but that he tosses off as "commonplace" (STUD, 1:19) and "obvious" (IDEN, 1:260). Ronald Knox, in his early Sherlockian parody of German scholarly methods, coined the term *Sherlockismus*, or "Sherlockism," for the more stylish of these deductions, the classic example being Holmes's epigrammatic reply to Inspector Gregory in "Silver Blaze":

> "Is there any point to which you would wish to draw my attention?"
> "To the curious incident of the dog in the night-time."
> "The dog did nothing in the night-time."
> "That was the curious incident," remarked Sherlock Holmes.
> (1:472)

Equally important are those gratuitous deductions that Doyle's South American readers called *Sherlockholmitos*, like the conclusions he draws from Watson's shoes in "A Scandal in Bohemia" (1:211) or from Henry Baker's hat in "The Blue Carbuncle" (1:331–32). As

Doyle explained, these displays of genius were intended, like Holmes's offhand allusions to other cases, to impress the reader with a sense of his power rather than to contribute to the plot (M&A, 100–101). The very prodigality with which Holmes tosses off his brilliant perceptions demonstrates how superior he is to the task he undertakes and the society he serves (Nordon, 221). In chapter 4 we considered the narrative sleights of hand needed to produce the plot effects of detective fiction. This chapter examines the fictionality of Holmes's reasoning processes and its effects on the assumptions we make about scientific and social order.

Although Doyle confessed himself a great fan of the detective stories of Poe and Gaboriau, he complained that the literary detective too often "obtains results without any obvious reason. That is not fair, that is not art."[1] In setting out to demonstrate his detective's cleverness in action, he took as his model Dr. Joseph Bell, his professor at the Royal Infirmary of Edinburgh. Bell used to dazzle the medical students with his ability to deduce details of his patients' profession, personality, and behavior from their accents, the mud on their shoes, or the shape of their bodies.[2] Doyle transferred this "eerie trick of spotting details" to Sherlock Holmes and, in the process, attempted to turn Bell's "fascinating but unorganized" abilities into "something nearer to an exact science" (M&A, 69). This "science," we should note, depends more on educated inferences than on specialized techniques. Holmes, it is true, is described as being expert in anatomy and a "first-class chemist" by Stamford, the friend who introduces him to Watson in a hospital laboratory where the sleuth has just discovered a test for identifying blood stains (STUD, 1:6–7). And Watson periodically alludes to the "chemical researches" that Holmes conducts in their Baker Street rooms (COPP, 1:437; IDEN, 1:262). But in actual practice, this kind of laboratory research is seldom shown to be of much direct help to him in solving mysteries. The stories popularize instead a general ideal of scientific observation and reasoning. We can recall from chapter 1 the prestige that scientific methods had gained during the nineteenth century and the personal importance of scientific standards of proof in Doyle's own crisis of faith. It was less important that Holmes be a scientist than that he be perceived as a scientific thinker, one who could fulfill his society's expectation that "more light and more justice" would be provided through the triumphant exercise of logic and scientific method (Nordon, 244).

The exact extent of Holmes's rationalism bears further inquiry. He appears to preach a strictly positivistic gospel of detection, one for which only the sternest empiricism and the most exacting logic will suffice. He possesses the scientist's skill at minute observation, what Watson describes as a "an extraordinary genius for minutiae" (SIGN, 1:110), for he understands that "there is nothing so important as trifles" when it comes to solving mysteries (TWIS, 1:319). He proclaims in *The Sign of Four* that he never guesses: "It is a shocking habit" (1:112). Theories are "bricks" that cannot be built without the "clay" of evidence (COPP, 1:437). He uses his own mistaken suspicion of gypsy involvement in "The Speckled Band" as the occasion to lecture Watson on "how dangerous it always is to reason from insufficient data" (1:368). Watson calls him "the most perfect reasoning and observing machine the world has seen" and admits that to such a mind, strong emotions like love would be as disruptive as "grit in a sensitive instrument, or a crack in one of his own high-power lenses" (SCAN, 1:209). Holmes rather ungratefully criticizes Watson at the beginning of "The Copper Beeches" for making lively tales out of his adventures instead of confining himself to "placing upon record that severe reasoning from cause to effect" that is their only "notable feature" (1:430).

If we contrast Holmes with the police, we can see that Doyle actually allows a wider scope for intuition and imagination in the private detective's reasoning. Lestrade's contemptuous dismissal of Holmes's deductions as mere "theories and fancies" in "Boscombe Valley" (1:280) is typical of the official reaction. The police fail to reason correctly precisely because they are too factual, too accepting of appearances. Lestrade errs by being shockingly "conventional" (STUD, 1:19); Gregory will never rise to great heights because he lacks imagination (SILV, 1:460). As Holmes tells Watson at the beginning of "A Case of Identity," police reports are so platitudinous that they conceal the "vital essence" of the crime; "a certain selection and discretion must be used in producing a realistic effect" (IDEN, 1:252).

This should remind us of the narrative manipulation necessary to make the plot of the investigation produce precisely those features required by the story of the crime. Although Holmes speaks elsewhere of "following docilely wherever fact may lead" (REIG, 1:557), his investigations are always guided by mental models—alternative "stories"—of how the crime could have occurred. He is able to determine which clues are relevant and to assemble them so as to reveal the solution, precisely because he does not expect facts to speak for themselves and is constantly testing them against hypotheses that his combination of observation, knowledge, and logic has already allowed him to form. Thus, we find that before he has even arrived at the Copper Beeches, he has already "devised seven separate explanations, each of which would cover the facts as far as we know them," and seeks further data to confirm which one is correct (1:439). Elsewhere he solves the mystery through a process of elimination, as when he determines that a former lover, not a spurned mistress, was responsible for Hatty Doran's disappearance in "The Noble Bachelor" (1:406). Charles Darwin, we should note, was also criticized by many contemporaries for providing only a "theory" of natural selection. Detection, like other studies that work backward from results to causes that by their very nature cannot be replicated, depends upon a leap of informed scientific imagination to construct a model whose adequacy is judged by its ability to predict or account for the effects in question. In the great majority of Holmes's cases, Doyle has artificially limited the possible explanations to fit the effects and allows the detective to guess correctly the first time or to eliminate alternatives easily. Watson seldom chronicles cases, like "The Five Orange Pips," for which solutions remained conjectural (1:289), and so Holmes's theories are triumphantly confirmed as fact—often by the perpetrators themselves—in denouement after denouement. His hypotheses thus attain a level of certainty that scientific theories, which by definition can be falsified but never proved unequivocally, can never claim.[3]

This effect is intensified by the kinds of rules his logic follows. Although Holmes and Watson both refer to his reasoning process as "deductive," it is actually closer to what the American philosopher Charles Peirce called "abduction" or "retroduction": moving backward from an effect to hypothesize about the situation(s) that could have caused it.[4] It is important to understand that this process, which Holmes describes as reasoning "analytically" in *A Study in Scarlet* (1:100), lacks the deduction's tautological accuracy. To see the difference, we can take two sets of propositions based on Holmes's claim that Henry Baker's hat proves that his wife has ceased to love him. The first represents the pattern typical of deduction:

Rule: Wives who have ceased to love their husbands will leave their hats unbrushed.
Case: Henry Baker's wife has ceased to love him.
Result: Henry Baker's hat has been left unbrushed.

In a syllogism like this one, if the "rule," or premise, is true, the result must be true. But this is in fact not the way Holmes reasons in "The Blue Carbuncle" and elsewhere. Abductive reasoning starts with the same kind of rule: Wives who have ceased to love their husbands will leave their hats unbrushed. But the case is different: Henry Baker has an unbrushed hat. Result: Henry Baker's wife has ceased to love him. Abductions like this one generate hypotheses about what might have produced the case, but there is no logical necessity that the particular hypothesis is true. Mrs. Baker could have been away on a visit or had a sprained hand, for instance. Holmes's virtual invincibility as a reasoner rests on the fact that Doyle has arranged the plots so that Holmes's abductions are almost always correct.

Holmes's vaunted "genius for minutiae" also rests in large part on successful inferences. Perception is guided by expectations. As he explains in "Silver Blaze," he is only able to see a telltale burned match buried in mud because his theory of how the crime had occurred led him to look for one there (1:466). Henry Baker's hat is meaningless to Watson, not because he cannot see it, but because he fails to reason from what he sees as Holmes does (BLUE, 1:330). Similarly, he does "not know where to look" for clues about Mary Sutherland's personality and background, so marks of her individuality remain "invisible" to him, despite his ability to describe her fashions in detail (IDEN, 1:260).

The power of Holmes's inferences, as well as their appeal to his Victorian audience, rests on the assumption that beneath the chaotic surface of life exists an underlying order to which all details can be linked by the trained observer. In the face of a universe that often seems incoherent and incomprehensible, Holmes affirms a fantasy of control by implying that all it takes to uncover nature's hidden order is a sufficient exercise of human intellect. Like many scientific essayists in the Victorian period, he demonstrates that even the most insignificant of everyday objects exemplify the working of scientific laws and thus testify to the systematic nature of reality (Clausen, 108; McConnell, 177; Ousby, 154). He puts it this way in his "Book of Life," quoted in *A Study in Scarlet*: "From a drop of water. . . a logician could infer the possibility of an Atlantic or a Niagara without having seen or heard of one or the other. So all life is a great chain, the nature of which is known whenever we are shown a single link of it" (1:14).

The metaphor here assumes an organic unity that Marshall McLuhan described as fundamental to nineteenth-century thought: "In an organic complex all parts have total relevance, not just *some* relevance to the whole."[5] The police fail because they expect a linear cause and effect; Holmes succeeds because he can re-create the network of relationships according to which what appears bizarre turns out to be the manifestation of a logical system. For Inspector Lestrade, and for Watson as well, clues can only have one meaning and so either point to an incorrect solution or to no solution at all. Holmes, in contrast, operates like a semiotician: he "reads" crimes like literary texts, as if they were systems of signs. The true significance of each sign is determined by its relation to others in a particular network of meaning. Because he can keep afloat a number of possible signifieds, or meanings, for each signifier, or clue, he is able eventually to recognize the one relationship capable of accounting for all the clues.[6]

Unlike most modern semioticians, however, Holmes operates as if the order he discovers is transcendent and natural, rather than arbitrary or artificially constructed. It is essential to the normative effects of his adventures that he appear to be simply demonstrating a reality that was there all the time, rather than discovering something novel or extraordinary. He points out that nothing could be stranger than the details of Hatty Doran's disappearance when viewed by Inspector Lestrade, for instance, and nothing more "natural" than the sequence of events as narrated by Hatty and anticipated by Holmes (NOBL, 1:406). The effect of Watson's repeated affirmations of how "ridiculously simple" (SCAN, 1:211) Holmes's conclusions are once explained or of Jabez Wilson's declaration that there was nothing clever after all in Holmes's ability to deduce that he had been a manual laborer, traveled to China, and recently undertaken a great deal of writing (REDH, 1:232) is to imply that there is little to detection except applied common sense and a trained eye. Holmes describes himself in "The Red-Headed League" as sharing with Watson a "love of all that is bizarre and outside the conventions and humdrum routine of everyday life" (1:230). Although such details provide the piquant stimulation his genius demands, they actually make crimes easier to solve because, by so obviously demanding explanation, they lead the scientific analyst most directly to the deeper conventions of behavior, according to which they are no longer bizarre. It is, after all, most often the anomalous detail or the discrepant case that alerts the scientist to the need for a stronger hypothesis that can explain it. "As a rule," Holmes explains, "the more bizarre a thing is the less mysterious it proves to be. It is your commonplace, featureless crimes which are really puzzling" (REDH, 1:241), presumably because they offer no distinctive traits that link them to the codes of meaning that order Holmes's world. Commonplace crimes are "unnatural" in this respect, since they appear to elude systematization, and Holmes prizes them precisely because they present the greatest challenge to his reasoning abilities: "It is usually in unimportant matters that there is a field for the observation, and for the quick analysis of cause and effect which gives the charm to an investigation" (IDEN, 1:253). In the end, however, all individual cases wind up being instances of more general types: Mary Sutherland's disappearing fiancé turns out to be a "trite" case of assumed identity (IDEN, 1:259), and Lord Robert St. Simon's disappearing wife has predictably flown with a previous husband. The interconnectedness of the "great chain" that constituted the Victorian vision of order ensures that every part has a fixed, limited, and identifiable position in the whole, so that the "ideal reasoner" could reconstruct a crime as completely as Cuvier could describe an entire animal from a single bone (FIVE, 1:300).

To bring his art to perfection, this ideal reasoner needs virtually encyclopedic knowledge. Shortly after their meeting in A Study in Scarlet, Watson is shocked to learn that Holmes knows nothing of the Copernican theory of the solar system. Holmes (quite erroneously) compares the brain to an attic of finite size and argues that since irrelevant information will crowd out and conceal what is necessary for a man's work, he stocks his brain only with what is immediately useful for detection. Thus, he possesses expert knowledge of poisons and mudstains, but no comprehensive understanding of botany or geology (1:11–12). As we have seen, his ignorance is repaired considerably in later stories as he is more fully fleshed out as a character, but he is still remarkable for his systematic study of things like cigar ash, tattoos, typewriter fonts, and the ways various trades shape the body.

Holmes admits in "The Five Orange Pips" that information not stored in a man's brain attic is not completely banished but rather kept in the "lumber-room of his library" for future reference; there he finds the American encyclopedia that identifies the Ku Klux Klan (1:302) or the directory of aristocratic families in which he looks up Lord Robert St. Simon in "The Noble Bachelor" (1:390). Holmes compiles his own customized indexes as well. He has adopted "a system of docketing all paragraphs concerning men and things"; the relevant facts about Irene Adler are found sandwiched between the biographies of a rabbi and a student of deep-sea fishes (SCAN, 1:215). One of his "ponderous commonplace books" of newspaper cuttings identifies the previous engineer to suffer at the hands of counterfeiters in "The Engineer's Thumb" (1:384), and he is busy "cross-indexing his records of crime" when John Openshaw arrives in "The Five Orange Pips" (1:290). Realizing that "there is a strong family resemblance about misdeeds" (STUD, 1:15), he carries around "a portable Newgate Calendar" in his mind (3GAR, 2:559) and can easily select the cases that match and explain new mysteries: the disappearance of Mary Sutherland's fiancé seems trite to him because it parallels cases in "Andover in '77" and "in the Hague last year" (1:259), and similar events in Aberdeen and in Munich lead him quickly to the explanation for Hatty Doran's disappearance (NOBL, 1:399). At a time when the knowledge explosion of the nineteenth century threatened to swamp the generally educated man in a tide of specialization, Holmes's mastery of so diverse an array of information would have been particularly reassuring.

Holmes shares with his brother Mycroft the mental abilities he describes in "The Bruce-Partington Plans." Mycroft "has the tidiest and most orderly brain, with the greatest capacity for storing facts, of any man living." He specializes in "omniscience" and serves as a kind of clearinghouse for government agencies, coordinating and "focusing" information from all sources to determine national policy (2:360). Holmes similarly knows how to access the relevant information from a vast array of knowledge and to select the exact constellation of facts necessary to solve a particular mystery. This confirms the argument that detection is essentially a puzzle-solving activity. The detective, unlike the literary critic, for instance, is not interested in celebrating the complexity or multiplicity of meanings in a text. For Holmes, there is only one correct interpretation. His task is to select this solution from "the finite and predetermined set of. . . clue-fitting" possibilities that his close observation and encyclopedic knowledge have provided him; he presides over what has been called a "ritual of reason," a repeated spectacle in which mystery, ambiguity, and complexity are reduced to logical order, thus demonstrating the sufficiency of rationality to master all problems.[7]

Notwithstanding Holmes's frequent demonstrations of how "obvious" his reasoning is, once explained, as readers we are not really in a position to match our wits with his. It is not just that we lack his command of fantastically specialized forms of knowledge, such as the texture of mud and dirt in all parts of England. Holmes operates in a world of ideal conformity and predictability, in which human bodies and behaviors are as easily classified as tattoos and mudstains. We need to give particular attention to the deterministic codes that allow Holmes to unlock the mysteries of human identity and motive, for these codes have significant ideological implications for the freedom and autonomy of those subject to them.

7

Detecting Difference

"You know my method," Holmes reminds Watson in "The Boscombe Valley Mystery." "It is founded upon the observation of trifles" (1:285). He goes on to explain how he was able to specify the "personality" of Charles McCarthy's murderer from the traces he left behind. The length of John Turner's stride reveals his height; its unevenness betrays his limp. The position of the head wound proves that he is left-handed, and detritus on the scene establishes his smoking habits. No wonder the iconic image of a magnifying glass is enough to specify the detective. He is first and foremost an observer of tracks and traces. He updates the hunter's ancient art of reconstructing the passage of his prey from the physical evidence left behind.

In her history of the detective novel, Alma Murch noted the considerable influence of the Indian tracking techniques described in James Fenimore Cooper's novels, the most famous of which was recalled in the title of Alexandre Dumas's *The Mohicans of Paris*. Hawkeye's disquisition in *The Last of the Mohicans* (1826) on how the minutest differences in footprints specify the identity of their owners can stand as a paradigm for the detective's ability to entrap criminals using the involuntary traces of their interaction with the physical environment (Murch, 40–41). By investigating the crime scene in "The Beryl Coronet," for instance, Holmes establishes not just the presence but also the movements of four different people—how long they had waited, how quickly they had moved and in what direction, where the scuffle between Arthur Holder and Sir George Burnwell took place (1:425–26). But individuality is ultimately ironic in the Holmesian universe. Unique traits are incriminating precisely because they are subject to rules of behavior or can be classified according to the systematic relationships that organize all physical evidence in an organically unified world. Personality only has meaning as the manifestation of regular laws of cause and effect that imprison clients as well as criminals in such a world. This chapter will probe some of the assumptions that construct the regularities of this system and their implications for conceptions of crime and social order.

The sophisticated techniques employed by forensic medicine and criminology have made the precise identification of evidence a commonplace of modern law enforcement. Much of Holmes's power derives from anticipating this ability to limit through specification, to detect minute differences where the layman sees only undifferentiated surfaces. Sensitivity to minor differences allows Holmes to distinguish the ash of 140 different kinds of tobacco, for instance (BOSC, 1:285). His expertise in dirt and soil types allows him to differentiate the gritty dust of the street from the fluffy house dust on Henry Baker's hat (BLUE, 1:332), to place John Openshaw in the southwest of England from the distinctive clay-and-chalk mixture on his shoes (FIVE, 1:291), or to tell that Helen Stoner has traveled to the train station in a dogcart over muddy roads because of the type and position of the stains on her sleeve (SPEC, 1:348). Even before the king arrives in "A Scandal in Bohemia" (1:212), Holmes links his prospective client to Bohemia on the basis of the watermarks on his stationery and determines that James Windibank and Hosmer Angel are the same person from 14 peculiarities of the typeface that both use (IDEN, 1:263).

Even more important in specifying individuality are distinctions built into the human body itself. Holmes is familiar with the significance of fingerprints (NORW, 1:697), established for the first time in the nineteenth century,[1] and professes enthusiasm (NAVA, 1:631) for the methods of the French criminologist Alphonse Bertillon, who developed indexes of body measurements intended to specify the "characteristic elements of individuality"[2] that would infallibly identify specific criminal offenders. What gives this evidence its power is the assumption that such physical signs are unconscious and difficult to dissemble, so that the body unwittingly incriminates itself. Hence, the analogies that have been drawn between this kind of clue and medical symptoms, "Freudian slips," and the trademark techniques of particular artists that, like their handwriting, are supposedly uncounterfeitable (Ginzberg, 86–88). But the paradox of individuality in the detective story is that it is interpretable precisely because it is not unique, because its marks are the product of predictable laws of behavior, just as specific medical symptoms are the product of specific diseases. In the Holmes stories this kind of predictability is extended in telling ways to account for a wide variety of human differences, in the process blurring the line between what was biologically determined and what was culturally acquired and allowing the detective story to construct status distinctions that it claims simply to reveal.

Nineteenth-century science based its authority on its ability to explain empirical phenomena as the result of uniform laws, rather than of intervention by capricious supernatural forces. Nature's regularity rested on predictable causes or common origins that could be reconstructed from their visible effects. Little wonder, given the century's interest in organic evolution, that efforts were made to systematize the physical evidence offered by the human body, to posit internal causes for external signs, and to organize difference into hierarchies. But it is also no surprise that in the process many preexisting prejudices about human difference laid claim to the authority of scientific law. The most notorious of these was the so-called science of racial difference, which sought to establish the innate inferiority of nonwhite and non-European groups by arguing that their closer physical resemblance to animals was a sign of their lower evolutionary status.[3] It played an important role in Cesare Lombroso's theory that criminals represented a distinct physical type that could be recognized by its atavistic resemblance to the ape. We see evidence of such views in the "low forehead, blunt nose, and prognathous jaw" that signal the moral degeneracy of Enoch Drebber, the Mormon villain in *A Study in Scarlet* (1:23). Jonathan Small, the revenger in *The Sign of Four*, is similarly described as "monkey-faced" (1:156), and Selden, the escaped convict in *The Hound of the Baskervilles*, possesses a "beetling forehead" and "sunken animal eyes" (2:114).

Lombroso's views were only a more particularized version of the widespread belief that the signs of a person's moral and intellectual nature were indelibly inscribed on the surface of the body, particularly on the face. Such an assumption owed much to the still vigorous popular tradition of physiognomy, which had for centuries claimed that internal character could be read from the size and shape of the facial features. Watson is guided by physiognomy when he interprets the King of Bohemia's "thick, hanging lip" and "long, straight chin" as suggesting "resolution pushed to the length of obstinacy" (SCAN, 1:213) or when he reads the signs of "unusual strength of. . . character" in the deeply lined, craggy features of John Turner's face (BOSC, 1:285), for instance. Phrenology updated such beliefs in the early nineteenth century by claiming that bumps and protrusions on particular parts of the head and face were linked to specific mental faculties or propensities. Holmes assumes this kind of correspondence when he concludes that Henry Baker is "highly intellectual" from the large size of his hat: "'It is a question of cubic capacity,' said he; 'a man with so large a brain must have something in it'" (BLUE, 1:331). Evolution had also inspired increased interest in heredity, although scientists lacked a satisfactory understanding of how traits were transmitted until well into the twentieth century (and even now we still debate the relative influences of genetics and environment in determining behavior). Many believed that not just physical resemblances, like the one that reveals Stapleton to be a Baskerville (2:121), but also moral tendencies could be determined by heredity, as does Helen Stoner when she opines that "violence of temper approaching to mania has been hereditary" in the men of the Roylott family (SPEC, 1:350) or Holmes when he concludes that the abnormal cruelty of the cockroach-smacking Rucastle child betrays a similar viciousness in his parents (COPP, 1:448).

What really renders the social universe transparent to Holmes is his ability to treat even the most commonplace details of dress and behavior as infallible signs of character or habit. We find this so convincing in part because it systematizes our own often unconscious assumptions that people can be judged by appearances. "Because science deals only with nonunique events," Accardo reminds us, "there can be no science of the individual" (13). In order to create the illusion of such a science, Doyle mutes the idiosyncracies that differentiate people and instead focuses on those traits that make them typical of particular social or ethnic groups. Consider language, for instance. The King of Bohemia's tortured use of English verbs identifies him as a native speaker of German before he appears; the conventional Australian cry of "cooee" tells Holmes that McCarthy was summoning a countryman in "Boscombe Valley." Appearance always proclaims class identity in the Holmes canon. Jabez Wilson "bore every mark of being an average commonplace British tradesman, obese, pompous, and slow" (REDH, 1:231). The "shiny, seedy coat," "red cravat," and "worn boots" that Holmes dons to investigate the Holder residence mark him as "a perfect sample of the class" of "common loafer" (BERY, 1:422). Mary Sutherland's costume gives her "a general air of being fairly well-to-do in a vulgar, comfortable, easy-going way" (IDEN, 1:260). In "The Blue Carbuncle" (1:340), the cut of the poultry salesman's whiskers proclaim as clearly as the pink racing form in his pocket that he can be drawn into a bet.

The fact that all but the last of these judgments are supplied not by Holmes but by Watson is significant; this is one situation where his lack of brilliance is no drawback. Watson is the voice of public convention. We discount Lord Robert St. Simon's judgment that the man he saw in the church was "quite a common-looking person" (NOBL, 1:396) because of his obvious snobbery; Watson's implicit air of social superiority does little to disqualify similar judgments that he makes, however. His prejudices seem innocuous (if they are even perceptible to us). And because Watson's initial characterizations of people are seldom significantly incorrect, they are more likely to appear simply commonsensical, resting on knowledge available to any reader. As a result, the entire project of stereotyping people by appearance is tacitly reaffirmed as natural and logical; Holmes merely carries this process to an extreme level of specialization, notwithstanding his occasional cautions to Watson about judging character from appearances (SIGN, 1:117; NORW, 1:695).

This is not to imply that real differences of appearance and behavior did not distinguish different social groups in Victorian England. The analysis of identity that Joseph Bell and Sherlock Holmes practiced was made significantly easier by the fact that class status was coded by distinctive styles of speech, dress, and body language, which Doyle would simply have taken for granted. We can doubtless identify similar stereotypes in our own society, and in any case, this signaling of character through external signs partakes of standard literary conventions. The acknowledgment that stereotypes may have some basis in fact takes on ideological significance in the Holmes stories (as well as in our own lives) when it slips into the assumption that individuals can be treated as nothing more than stereotypes, completely predictable from visual signs and limited to the kinds of social power and ability that prejudice assigns to that type. In the exaggeration and simplification of effects that fiction often requires, Doyle's unconscious assumptions about social difference take on the intensity of law. The specificity and analytical rigor Holmes claims for his detections provide these prejudices with a scientific justification and vastly widen the scope of behavior that inescapably types a person.

In a world where predictability means control, however, we find that in practice all groups are not submitted to the same degree of typing. Holmes's coding of individuals operates differently for different classes, in ways that tacitly justify the greater power and privilege of the higher classes over the lower ones. Take, for example, Holmes's skill in reading what Joseph Bell referred to as "the sign-manuals of labour" and "the stains of trade."[4] It was Bell's startling ability to infer his patients' trades from the marks left on their bodies—to identify a linoleum worker from the dermatitis on her fingers or a cobbler from the worn trouser knee where he rested his lapstone, for instance—that formed the basis for the systematic skills with which Doyle would endow his "scientific detective."[5] In dismissing Watson's survey of Mary Sutherland's fashions as irrelevant, Holmes lectures him on the importance of "details" like sleeves, thumbnails, and boot laces: "My first glance is always at a woman's sleeve. In a man it is perhaps better first to take the knee of the trouser" (IDEN, 1:260). He correctly infers that she is a typist from the traces left by resting her arms against the table edge, just as he confirms his suspicions about Jabez Wilson's assistant by discerning the muddy condition of his knees (REDH, 1:242). Presumably, clothing could be changed to conceal one's background; not so with work that deforms the body itself, as so much physical labor is alleged to do. Wilson's right hand has been permanently enlarged by his early carpentry work (REDH, 1:232), for example. Unlike the "great unobservant public," Holmes can identify the weaver by his tooth (notched from biting off thread) or the compositor by his left thumb, calloused from sliding type off his composing stick (COPP, 1:431).

And yet his sweeping claim that a man's calling is "plainly revealed" by his fingernails, callouses, and clothing (STUD, 1:15) is clearly much truer of the working than of the middle and upper classes. Where the lower classes tend to be indelibly "stained," to use Bell's term, by their collisions with the world of objects, the higher classes are marked from the inside out, not by what they have done but by what they "are." Good "breeding," as the term suggests, is a process whereby signs of moral and intellectual superiority are carried through blood and internalized in their faces, heads, and the ways they carry their bodies. A gentleman like John Openshaw invariably manifests his gentility through "something of refinement and delicacy in his bearing" (FIVE, 1:291). Notwithstanding his grotesque deformity as the beggar Hugh Boone, Neville St. Clair is in his own person a "refined-looking man" (TWIS, 1:324). Violet Hunter's acquired skills as a governess are less important to Jephro Rucastle than her possession of "the bearing and deportment of a lady," although whether this is because he is really concerned with her fitness to rear "a child who may some day play a considerable part in the history of the country" or simply wants a credible double to impersonate his daughter Alice is another question (COPP, 1:433). The intangible signs of class refinement naturally enough also outweigh more grossly physical signs in determining status. Violet Smith, from "The Solitary Cyclist" in the *Return of Sherlock Holmes*, has spatulate fingers that could belong to either a typist or a musician, but Holmes knows that the "spirituality" of her face is such that "the typewriter does not generate" (SOLI, 1:728). We might also consider the difference between a genteel bearing and the military air that allows Holmes to identify various former soldiers (for instance, STUD, 1:18; GREE, 1:599). Their characteristic posture and self-control are clearly the product of training and routine. In a telling anecdote, Joseph Bell explained how he determined from a patient's "swagger" and general air that he must have been a soldier, only to have him deny it. Upon having the man seized and stripped, however, Bell discovered that he had been branded as a military deserter.[6]

This is appropriate, for the conformity of the lower classes, induced by their inability to resist the pressures of their environment, is always implicitly incriminating in the realm of Holmesian detection. In contrast, the internalized gentility of the higher classes is usually a source of power. Making a genteel bearing the product of good breeding, moreover, implies that it is not simply a learned trait but is in some sense innate and uncounterfeitable, almost a biological essence. The lower classes are thus doubly penalized, treated as helplessly malleable by the conditions of their labor and physically incapable of that intrinsic gentility without which they can never hope to transcend the limits imposed by their station, no matter how much they might improve their material lot in life.

The tendency in these stories to treat the lower classes as more thoroughly subject to their own physicality or more closely identified with bodily functions echoes a pattern common to the late Victorian imagination, which associated the poor with dirt, animality, and pollution, and linked manual laborers and servants metaphorically as well as literally to their socially and physically "low" work. The genteel classes, literally insulated from dirty and undignified physical labor, were figuratively characterized by higher, immaterial traits like intellect, spirituality, and bearing.[7] The most significant implications of this metaphorical alignment of the lower classes with the physical and the higher with the intellectual become clear if we measure the relative freedom these respective groups exercise in the Holmes stories. The lower-class characters are not only marked by physical signs that cannot be concealed, but they are also less in control of their bodies and their secrets and are more easily manipulated by Holmes, who can disarm their most subtle resistance to authority. The trick of dealing with lower-class people, he explains to Watson in *The Sign of Four*, is to prevent them from realizing the value of what they know: "Never. . . let them think that their information can be of the slightest importance to you. If you do they will instantly shut up like an oyster. If you listen to them under protest, as it were, you are very likely to get what you want" (SIGN, 1:157). Holmes, disguised as a groom, spends an afternoon gossiping in the stables behind Irene Adler's villa and succeeds in learning what he wants to know about her, but only after being compelled to listen to the biographies of half a dozen other completely irrelevant neighborhood people as well (SCAN, 1:219). In "The Blue Carbuncle," he learns the name of the poultry salesman by complimenting the landlord of the Alpha Inn and then tricks the recalcitrant tradesman, Breckenridge, into revealing the source of the goose by allowing him to win a bet on whether it was town- or country-bred (1:338, 340). In several stories the "agony" or personal columns of the daily papers (which we find him reading at the start of "The Engineer's Thumb," 1:372) often afford him a way of eavesdropping on the secrets of the general public; he describes this source in "The Three Garridebs" as his "favorite covert for putting up a bird" (2:553)—that is, a place where criminal activity is driven into the open, at least to the eyes of the skilled hunter who preys on the secrets of the unsophisticated.

More genteel characters exercise greater control over their bodies and their emotions. Mary Holder, whose face reveals to Watson her "immense capacity for self-restraint" (BERY, 1:419), successfully conceals her love affair and her complicity in the theft of the Beryl Coronet from the uncle who assumes he knows her so well. Aristocrats generally constitute "a caste who do not lightly show emotion" and seldom expose the "natural man" behind the "aristocratic mask" (SECO, 1:911, 904). We get a glimpse of this in the rigid reserve maintained by the offended St. Simon at the end of "The Noble Bachelor." Powerful men like Alexander Holder can be driven to revealing in their absurd physical contortions the "symptoms" that tell Holmes they are prospective clients (BERY, 1:408), but only under the extreme stress of both personal and professional catastrophe. In later stories, we find that gentlemen sometimes fly into rages, but are capable of reducing the "hot flame of anger" to "frigid" indifference by virtue of their "supreme self-command," especially when confronted by Holmes's even greater coolness and self-assurance (THOR, 2:570; DEVI, 2:436; SHOS, 2:646). By contrast, the "rat-faced" hotel attendant James Ryder collapses in a sniveling heap when confronted with his theft of the Blue Carbuncle; Holmes tellingly describes him as not having "blood enough" to commit a felony with impunity (1:342). James Windibank, a somewhat more respectable traveling salesman, similarly shrinks "like one who is utterly crushed" when exposed as Hosmer Angel, but recovers enough of his assurance to defy Holmes with a sneer at the end of the story (IDEN, 1:264–65).

Genteel and aristocratic criminals normally carry their social distinction into their crimes. The glamorous Sir George Burnwell "is one of the most dangerous men in England." No sniveling for him: he threatens Holmes with a bludgeon after the detective has (characteristically) tricked his valet into incriminating him as the thief of the Beryl Coronet (1:425, 429). And of course the bank robber John Clay, a duke's grandson with an Eton and Oxford education, winds up at the head of his "profession" (REDH, 1:245). In what Michel Foucault has called the "aesthetic rewriting of crime" in nineteenth-century Europe, the common people were increasingly viewed as incapable of truly "great" crimes. These became the province of the intellectually and socially superior (68–69). "When a clever man turns his brains to crime it is the worst of all"; for instance, when a physician like the impoverished aristocrat Dr. Grimesby Roylott goes wrong, "he is the first of criminals" (SPEC, 1:362, 364). Although Holmes often laments that "the days of the great cases are past" (COPP, 1:431), he does find worthy foes in the audacious and intelligent Stapleton of *The Hound of the Baskervilles*, or in Baron Gruner of "The Illustrious Client," "a real aristocrat of crime" who shares Holmes's artistic temperament, the sign of that "complex mind" that "all great criminals" possess (ILLU, 2:467–68). These men yield first place to Professor James Moriarty, the mathematical genius and Napoleon of crime who can serve as Holmes's archenemy because he is his only genuine equal

"'Have Mercy!' He Shrieked": Original Sidney Paget illustration for "The Blue Carbuncle."

Reproduced courtesy of the Metropolitan Toronto Reference Library.

(FINA, 1:645). It goes without saying that such criminal geniuses are free from the genetic stigmata of crime that mark their underlings. Stapleton is "clean-shaven" and "prim-faced" (HOUN, 2:56), and John Clay's white hands and boyish looks allow him to masquerade as a philanthropist (REDH, 1:248). Moriarty's manner strikes Holmes as "reptilian," but his features are "ascetic" rather than animalistic (FINA, 1:646–47).

And how does Holmes himself fit into these patterns of class stereotyping? We earlier considered the way his evasiveness functions as a plot device to prolong suspense. Now we can also view it as a sign of his social and intellectual superiority. He need not bother to turn the lamp away from his own face to spotlight his client's, as he does when John Openshaw arrives in "The Five Orange Pips," because that "weary, heavy-lidded expression" that Watson so often describes as veiling "his keen and eager nature" (ENGR, 1:373) ensures that he will give none of his own thoughts away. His startling success at disguise offers even more dramatic opportunities for concealment. Indeed, his skill at counterfeiting himself makes Holmes, the reader of all social codes, appear to be subject to none. As we have seen, he is the master of the signs of class and vocation, able to adopt the clothing, gait, and manner of the groom, the loafer, or the clergyman. And although the value of physiognomical signs and medical symptoms rests in their supposedly involuntary and unconscious betrayal of the bearer's condition, Holmes easily imitates the decrepit, wrinkled lassitude of an aging opium addict at the beginning of "Twisted Lip." When he reappears in "The Empty House" disguised as a hunchback bookseller, he has taken a foot off his height (EMPT, 1:667), and in "The Dying Detective" he convinces Dr. Watson that he is in the death throes of an obscure tropical disease (DYIN, 2:386).

The very success of these masquerades raises questions about his claim that deceit is impossible where the detective's observation and analysis of individuals are concerned (STUD, 1:14). If the signs that betray one's class or character are truly infallible, how can Holmes so easily counterfeit social identity? For that matter, the fact that a change of clothing and a little makeup can transform the genteel Neville St. Clair into the completely convincing street beggar Hugh

Boone raises questions about whether social superiority really rests on anything more intrinsic than appearance. We will consider the implications of his story in more detail in the following chapter; for now, we should note that even in disguise, St. Clair gives evidence of his intellectual superiority in the witty repartee that sets him apart from "the common crowd of mendicants" and helps ensure his financial success (TWIS, 1:315). It is also significant that he, like Holmes in the great majority of his disguises, imitates someone of lower social status. Slumming by the upper classes is always less socially threatening than its opposite—the attempt of the vulgar to pass for something they are not—because no real social power is at risk. Given the logic of social coding in the Sherlock Holmes stories, the lower classes are by definition less complicated; their identities consist of little more than the physical effects of their work or their experience. Such external signs can be easily imitated by their betters, whose rich emotional and mental complexity cannot in turn be duplicated by anyone not to the manor born. In this sense, Sherlock Holmes, the master of disguise, offers only the most extreme example of the way social and intellectual superiority permits the selective transcendence of coding and the control it signifies.

In his study of shifting paradigms for crime and punishment in the nineteenth century, Foucault described the transition from a legal system based on physical punishment to one based upon reform through imprisonment, and from control through violence to control through information. As power—conceived less as force than as the prerogative to define what counts as reality—becomes more anonymous in the modern state, Foucault argued, those most subject to it become less able to elude it. They are in effect controlled by having all aspects of their identities subject to surveillance and measured against behavioral norms (192–93). Nowhere was this kind of surveillance more desired than in the modern city, the anonymity of which threatened to shield wrongdoers from punishment and left everyone potentially vulnerable to the unpredictability of strangers. One response to such anxiety in France was the development of what were called *physiologies*, illustrated handbooks that supposedly enabled the public to determine the profession, life-style, and moral character of strangers from their external appearance; another was the contemporaneous rise of detective fiction, which similarly reassured the public that the individual's traces were readable and could not be concealed in the crowd.[8] At the beginning of "A Case of Identity," Holmes's fantasy of flying over London and taking off the roofs to "peep at the queer things which are going on" (1:251) brilliantly realizes the detective's role in this kind of power structure: he is the unseen seer from whose glance no deviance can escape. In "The Copper Beeches" he pronounces the country to be more dangerous than the city precisely because private estates could shield wrongdoing from the scrutiny that restrains criminality, although it is telling that the examples he gives (drunken violence and child abuse) are explicitly associated with the lower classes (1:438–39). Most often, it is not direct surveillance but the detective's mastery of social coding that defines and polices the boundaries of the "normal" in this society. At the same time that his gaze individualizes and makes anonymity impossible, it also "effects a reduction in the value of individuality, which, in the tell-tale clues through which it is revealed, is defined as a statistical effect rather than as the product of a unique psyche."[9] As Holmes himself puts it, "While the individual man is an insoluble puzzle, in the aggregate he becomes a mathematical certainty" (SIGN, 1:175), for the laws of human behavior are as regular as the propositions of Euclid (STUD, 1:14).

The detective's real ideological power to invent and enforce social conformity by interpreting appearance is masked by the rhetoric of amateurism and artistry with which Holmes characterizes his business. Being unofficial, disassociated from the formal power structure, actually increases his authority, just as it increases his effectiveness, since he has nothing personal to gain from detection. He has a positive aversion to publicity and an abhorrence of "popular applause" (DEVI, 2:418); he spurns the offer of a knighthood when he recovers the eponymous Bruce-Partington Plans because he "play[s] the game for the game's own sake," not for public acclaim (2:363). He most effectively implements a particular class agenda by appearing to have none, to pursue solely what is obviously right and fair, to become involved simply because "it's every man's business to see justice done" (CROO,

1:574). Because he is "no official agent" (BOSC, 1:286), he can allow wrongdoers like John Turner or James Ryder to escape punishment in the name of a higher good, thus serving as "the last court of appeal" (FIVE, 1:291) in more ways than one. He informs Watson "without affectation" that a client's standing in society is of less importance to him than the interest of the case (NOBL, 1:389). Jabez Wilson seeks him out as someone known to be "good enough to give advice to poor folk who were in need of it" (REDH, 1:240). Although we see him "pocketing his fee" from lower-class clients gladly enough in his early *Study in Scarlet* days (1:16), by the beginning of the *Adventures* he usually expects only reimbursement of his expenses. His profession is its own reward, as he tells Helen Stoner; he is "amply repaid" by having "unique" experiences such as that offered by the Red-Headed League, although he is not above accepting "souvenirs" like Irene's picture or gold trinkets from those who can easily afford them (SPEC, 1:348; REDH, 1:.249; SCAN, 1:229; IDEN, 1:252).

Holmes's role in influencing social order is also concealed by his stance as the unofficial but expert administrator of information. His brother Mycroft is of course the exemplar of this new professional order in which the highest status is accorded to the most purely intellectual work. Sherlock describes him as the real power behind the British government by virtue of his ability to order facts so that their relationship creates meaning and leads to action (BRUC, 2:360). Mycroft carries to comic lengths his aversion to action itself; his calling in life, as he explains to Sherlock, is to render expert opinions from an armchair, not "to run here and run there, to cross-question railway guards, and lie on my face with a lens to my eye." These kinds of menial tasks he leaves to his younger brother to take care of in "The Bruce-Partington Plans" (2:363). Notwithstanding his more active role in amassing information, Sherlock, like Mycroft, is empowered more by his immaterial genius than by his physical labors. At its best, his reasoning power becomes a kind of intuition (REDH, 1:243), something that must be innate and not simply acquired through hard work. We have noted how seldom his chemical researches play any direct role in solving crimes, and for the real dirty work of stakeouts and spying, he usually employs others, like the band of street urchins known as the Baker Street Irregulars (SIGN, vol. 1, chap. 8) or the various assistants he uses in later stories (Cartwright in HOUN, 2:108, or Mercer in CREE, 2:599, for instance). Sherlock Holmes is depicted as a thinker, not a worker, someone whose only "business" is to know what others do not (BLUE, 1:341). Standing above the economic fray, he plays the role of the specialist who simply reasons his way to preexisting truths.

Holmes also resembles the aesthetes of the 1890s, not just in the amoral intellectual curiosity he brings to his investigations but also in the artist's pose he assumes. The "art for art's sake" movement explicitly rejected the mid-Victorian assumption that art should deliver uplifting moral messages; as Oscar Wilde responded in his "Preface" to *The Picture of Dorian Gray* (1891), "There is no such thing as a moral or an immoral book. Books are well written, or badly written. That is all."[10] The aesthetes declared that political or social content was irrelevant to art; a work's intrinsic beauty should be the sole criterion for its evaluation. Although perhaps less morally exacting than the Victorians, we find ourselves in the 1990s still enmeshed in versions of this debate over whether and how an artwork's ideological content affects its merits. To those who insist that eternal aesthetic standards should be the only measure of artistic value, critics have responded by pointing out that a work need not deliver overtly political messages to have political implications. Insofar as works of art create selective views of reality that rest on unstated assumptions about the naturalness and logic of certain social arrangements and human behaviors, they take ideological positions that are neither eternal nor universal; they simply do not acknowledge the selectivity of their vision. Conceptions of beauty themselves often depend on a work's relationship to preexisting social and aesthetic conventions, conventions rendered invisible by appeals to the work's intrinsic artistic value. By likening detection to an art form ("an impersonal thing—a thing beyond myself") and himself to one who "loves art for its own sake" as Holmes does in "The Copper Beeches" (1:429-30) and by quoting the line that "the man is nothing, the work is all" (REDH, 1:251) from the French novelist Flaubert, known for his highly polished and impersonal style, Holmes seems to absolve himself from any personal responsibility for the order he discovers in his pursuit of intellectually beautiful solutions to intricate problems.

Whether depicted as the product of artistic insight or intellectual rigor, Holmes's detections have the same effect: they purport to view social relations from a standpoint above or outside partisan interests. Thus, the differences they assume in the freedoms and abilities of different classes are presented as neutral truths waiting to be perceived or discovered, rather than fictional constructions shaped by unconscious biases about the sources of privilege. Distinctions that may have been acquired as a result of historical accident or economic luck re-emerge in the fiction as in some unspecified way innate or intrinsic to particular groups, natural rather than cultural, the cause rather than the effect of their social superiority. The complete predictability of human behavior that empowers the detective limits the lower classes far more than higher. The quasi-biological determinism assumed in the stories reaffirms the status quo by providing a physical rationale for the lower classes' subordination to material conditions and provides an intangible basis for the higher classes' claims to transcend them.

Authors seldom set out to write fiction to support what they would consider a specific political agenda. Like Doyle, they unconsciously reproduce a world that seems natural to them, given their historically and economically determined position in it. But if writers are innocent, the fictions they create seldom are. Ideology is the power to present one's own values as part of the neutral backdrop of reality, to construct a vision so compelling that it is difficult to imagine alternative worlds. The appeal of detective fiction in particular rests on its ability to simplify and exaggerate for artistic effect, to provide readers with the fantasy of order and control that they desire. Arthur Conan Doyle's genius for extrapolating a world of ideal predictability from common behavioral signs brilliantly satisfies this craving in the Sherlock Holmes stories, but at the expense of mystifying the sources of social power. As we examine the *Adventures* more closely in the following chapters, we will see how their plotting of crime and punishment also presents certain relationships and values as natural and empowers some members of society at the expense of others.

8

Plotting Social Order

"Whodunit?" Our slang expression for a detective story assumes that the real story of every crime lies in the guilty individual who perpetrates it, just as the solitary figure of the detective assures us that disorder meets its match in the brilliant individual. Muted in both cases is the possibility that crime and disorder might have economic or historical roots in an unfair distribution of power, wealth, or opportunity, or that the guilt for wrongdoing might be at least in part collective rather than entirely individual. Treating detection as an intellectual puzzle, a mystery that ends when the wrongdoer is identified and needs no legal follow-up to complete its meaning, further isolates the wrongs done from their social contexts. As we saw in chapter 5, the detective story was made possible largely by a shift in the attitudes of the middle classes toward crime and the police. Their gains in wealth and position gave them an investment in social order and a desire for protection. We should not wonder, then, that these fictions so often work to suppress any doubts about the legitimacy of middle- class authority and to banish whatever fears of insecurity and instability they may temporarily arouse.

Significantly, the Sherlock Holmes stories for the most part do not focus on what were perceived at the time as the most serious threats to social order in later Victorian and Edwardian society. We catch no glimpses of the white-slavery sensations of the 1880s or of the anarchists and other terrorists who disturbed the peace in the closing decades of the century for political reasons, although the (always foreign) secret societies that figure in several stories (like the Ku Klux Klan in "The Five Orange Pips") may owe something to such groups.[1] The increasing masses of under- or unemployed urban slum dwellers, those "dangerous classes" whose revolutionary potential was a persistent source of anxiety in later Victorian London, remain virtually invisible. Instead, wrongdoing tends to be focused inward, on threats to the security and reputation of individuals and families and to the codes of conduct that underpin middle-class power. As Watson observes at the beginning of "The Blue Carbuncle," half of the preceding *Adventures* have involved no legal crime; rather, Holmes's cases are most often presented as "striking" and "bizarre" little problems (1:328) that trace disorder back to the moral failures of individuals—to their illicit desire for wealth, to their betrayal of the mores appropriate to their class or of the loyalties that ensure social stability. This tendency to treat crime as a moral issue derives in part from the fact that the middle classes had advanced their claims to social prestige in the nineteenth century by linking social power to evidence of appropriate conduct, rather than to hereditary wealth and position. In turn, the fulfillment of such class ideals rationalized the possession of wealth, so we can anticipate that in these stories the issue of whether a person deserves to enjoy property will often be translated into terms of morality or conduct.

The chief locus of anxiety in these early stories is more often than not the family circle; for John Cawelti, the pervasive pattern of Holmes and Watson departing from the snug comforts of their Baker Street rooms to invade the dark and stormy world outside symbolizes the vulnerability of middle-class domesticity that so often lies submerged in these plots (Cawelti, 97). The sources of internal threat are various: the sins of the fathers being visited on their children (in "The Five Orange Pips" or "Boscombe Valley," for instance), the violation of paternal responsibility by greedy father figures ("A Case of Identity," "The Speckled Band," or "The Copper Beeches"), the surrender of class ideals to crass profit motives ("The Twisted Lip"), or sexual passion that overrides filial loyalties ("The Beryl Coronet"). The roots of weakness are most often traced outward to opposite ends of the social scale, to dishonest servants and unworthy aristocrats ("A Scandal in Bohemia," "The Red-Headed League," "The Blue Carbuncle," "The Beryl Coronet," "The Noble Bachelor"). As we might expect in a social universe where status depends upon maintaining one's respectability, however, the most pervasive plot motif in the Holmes stories involves the threat of scandal and the concealment of secret unworthiness—imprudent love affairs, illicit financial dealings, foreign plots, and criminal intrigues. Whether blackmail is literally involved or not, the truth about a person's identity is frequently held hostage by the importance of maintaining a respectable appearance in a society in which a good reputation was the middle and upper classes' most valuable commodity.

Holmes and Watson are perfectly situated to deal with such threats. Watson's circumspection about not telling the real story behind "The Speckled Band" until after Helen Stoner's death (1:346) is typical of the care he exercises throughout the canon to protect the secrets and conceal the real names of Holmes's clients. In a late Victorian England rocked by public scandals (Ousby, 165), Holmes's vigilance not just in protecting his clients' privacy but in allowing them to escape official punishment (as he does in "A Case of Identity," "Boscombe Valley," "The Twisted Lip," "The Blue Carbuncle," and "The Beryl Coronet") would have been a particularly reassuring benefit of his extralegal status. Public confidence in the competence of the police had been undermined by a scandal at Scotland Yard in 1877 and by their failure to prevent the Trafalgar Square riots of 1886; Holmes's contempt for their abilities would have struck a responsive chord in many readers. His brilliance allows him to achieve what they cannot, but his discretion in dealing with "delicate" issues is his greatest attraction. Holmes's later services to the queen, the pope, and various other monarchs and high government officials not only testify to his genius but also suggest that the security of the state depends upon being able to keep the affairs of the powerful a secret from their own people.

Holmes's very eccentricities give him unique advantages in such situations. The conventionality of the police, their commonsense practicality and prosaic imagination, limit their effectiveness. Holmes lives outside conventional relationships in a society in which romantic love and family ties are so often shown to be a source of vulnerability and disorder. He does not share the orthodox views and superstitions that blind others to the real sources of crime, and he is sufficiently aloof from high society that his dangerous command of its secrets poses no immediate embarrassments. His disinterestedness draws the threat from his command of secrets (Clausen, 114; Most, 343; Cawelti, 95). And notwithstanding his constant efforts to correct wrongdoing, he never questions the bases of social order in any fundamental way. No revolutionary realignments of social power are necessary to solve this society's problems; no centralized bureaucracies are required to restore and maintain order. He calls upon individuals to reform their behavior, to be more worthy of the duties entailed by their position in society, not to repudiate existing values (Nordon, 259). If he often evades the letter of the law in order to enforce a private, genteel code of honor (Ousby, 168), this private code ultimately upholds essentially the same class prerogatives as those protected by the legal system.

The sources of wrongdoing and social power in each of *The Adventures of Sherlock Holmes* will receive individual analysis in the following pages. Although I have grouped the stories by similarities in the motives or methods they involve, certain other issues cut across them: the significance of class identities and values, the intertwining of property and reputation, Holmes's essentially conservative role in maintaining the status quo. What is perhaps the most important common element in his *Adventures*—sexual passions and the women who are considered to incite them—must receive some mention in this chapter; however, I will reserve those stories in which gender concerns are more central for separate consideration in chapter 9.

74

CRIMINAL ACTIONS: "THE RED-HEADED LEAGUE," "THE ENGINEER'S THUMB," AND "THE BLUE CARBUNCLE"

Given the tremendous influence of Sherlock Holmes on later detective traditions, it is striking that the crimes that define the murder mystery and the cops-and-robbers adventure are actually relatively rare among Holmes's adventures. Crimes of passion are more common than crimes of calculation, and cases involving impersonal criminal acts— that is, where the perpetrators have no personal motives for attacking their victims—are also the exception rather than the rule. Not greed itself, but its corrosive effects on human relationships, is the most common locus of anxiety. With the significant exception of Moriarty's crime network, professional criminals like the bank-robbing John Clay or the coiners in "The Engineer's Thumb" appear infrequently in the earlier Holmes adventures and degenerate into hackneyed gangster stereotypes in late stories like "The Mazarin Stone" or "The Three Gables." And, like Holmes, Moriarty is more of a thinker than an actor, a genius distanced from crime in a managerial function rather than a common thief. Even in the *Adventures* that involve criminal conspiracies, what remains fictionally most memorable is less the crime itself than its surrounding complications: the fantastic eccentricity of the Red-Headed League, Hatherly's romantic escape from the coining press, the business of Henry Baker's hat. As readers, we, like Holmes, usually prefer the striking and the bizarre to the merely criminal.

The case of "The Red-Headed League" presents itself initially as just such an incident "outside the conventions and humdrum routine of everyday life" that Holmes and Watson so relish (REDH, 1:230). As Holmes later explains, of course, "the more bizarre a thing is the less mysterious it proves to be" (1:241), since its very eccentricity signals its deviance from the norm. This tale aptly illustrates Franco Moretti's claim that in the detective story, "innocence is conformity; individuality, guilt." The perfect crime is the one that anyone could have committed; detective fiction exists "to dispel the doubt that guilt might be impersonal, and therefore collective and social." Eccentricity is inherently culpable; it signals a desire to nourish some private core of individuality that will not conform to community standards. Secrets are by definition criminal, and it is the detective's task to make privacy impossible by laying all human behavior open for scrutiny and classification (Moretti, 135–36). The idea that a lower-class man like Jabez Wilson could be rewarded instead of incriminated by his physical peculiarities is the first tip-off that something may be criminally wrong with this situation. As is often the case in the Holmes canon, the instigation for the eccentric behavior is allegedly foreign: the benefactor of red-haired men is supposedly one Ezekiah Hopkins, late of Lebanon, Pennsylvania. Foreigners are always treated as exotics by Doyle, as if to imply that the infection of British normalcy is more plausible when it comes from exposure to alien contagions. In fact, of course, the colorful Mr. Wilson is only a pawn in a game manipulated by the aristocratic John Clay, alias Vincent Spaulding. The task of copying out the *Encyclopaedia Britannica* is simply a fool's errand designed to get Wilson out of his shop so that Clay and his accomplice can complete their tunnel to the bank. Wilson is really expendable for both Clay and Holmes. Once he has served the thieves' purposes, he ceases to be of any interest; he is more significant for his absence than for his presence, and his sole claim to distinction is dissolved along with the Red-Headed League itself (Priestman, 88). Likewise, once his physical features have afforded Holmes the opportunity for one of his bravura deductions about character and his odd employment has titillated the detective's (and the reader's) imagination, the "not over-bright pawn-broker" (1:249) simply drops out of the story, which then moves on to the real confrontation between social and intellectual equals.

The other signal of underlying disorder in this story is the relationship between labor and money. In a capitalist society, supply and demand supposedly regulate wages. As Moretti argued, "suspicion often originates from a violation of the law of exchange between equivalent values: anyone who pays more than a market price or accepts a low salary can only be spurred by criminal motives" (139). Holmes reports that as soon as he learned that Wilson's assistant accepted half wages for the job, he suspected ulterior motives behind his desire for employment (REDH, 1:250). Similarly, only the most extreme eccentricity could justify a man in offering a salary of £4 a week for "purely nominal services" like copying out of an encyclopedia; Wilson is right to suspect a hoax or fraud behind it (1:237–38). Sure enough, this salary turns out to be merely the "lure" that Clay correctly predicts will entrap a man like Wilson (1:250). Holmes reinforces the legitimacy of this value system and (in a move that we will see is typical of his treatment of lower-class characters) makes light of Wilson's distress at losing his sinecure, telling him he has no grievance against a situation that has enriched him not only by £30 but also by "the minute knowledge" he has gained "on every subject which comes under the letter A." For Holmes, Wilson's humiliation is merely a "refreshingly unusual" problem that affords him and Watson a good laugh. He correctly surmises that "graver issues" are at stake than Wilson's loss of face or income (1:240).

John Clay turns out to be an effective first draft of the criminal genius that Doyle would later create in James Moriarty. Both have "remarkable" intellects that have put them at the head of their profession (REDH, 1:245) and make them fitting opponents with whom Holmes has personal scores to settle (REDH, 1:249). As befits their intelligence and class standing, both successfully elude the law by concealing their illegal occupations: Moriarty masquerades as a college professor turned academic coach (FINA, 1:645), and the aristocratic Clay is free to carry out the charitable activities (raising money for an orphanage) that one expects from a man of his station. Signs of their criminal activity abound, but no one can catch them red-handed and thus prove their guilt. Presumably, it is not just Clay's inaccessibility that protects him from apprehension but his aristocratic lineage as well: a duke's grandson has nothing to fear from police who can offer only circumstantial evidence that he is the mastermind behind a string of forgeries and thefts (1:245). Although we are expected to find somewhat ludicrous his insistence on his aristocratic dignity after he is captured (he tells the police to keep their "filthy" hands off him and to address him as "sir," as befits one with "royal blood" in his veins), we are also supposed to respect the "utmost coolness" with which he accepts his defeat and to take seriously Holmes's compliments to him on the ingenuity of his red-headed scheme (1:249). His reserve and intelligence are the signs of a class superiority that has helped protect him from apprehension for so long; appropriately, it is when he stoops to the physical labor that would otherwise be considered far beneath him that the dirty knees of his trousers give him away to Holmes, just as clothing betrays the secrets of so many other workers to the detective's expert eye.

Clay is only one of many aristocratic rogues targeted in these stories as sources of danger and disruption. Aristocrats' monopoly on wealth and power had traditionally been the focus of middle-class resentment, and implying that they were morally unworthy of their privileges was an effective way to advance middle-class claims for their own superiority. John Clay's ambiguous sexuality may represent one such form of attack on upper-class character: his pierced ears, "white, almost womanly hand," and his camaraderie with a lower-class sidekick "lithe and small like himself" might have hinted at a homosexual relationship in the 1890s (1:240, 248; Priestman, 89). And yet, while we will certainly find evidence of this tactic in other Holmes stories, by the later Victorian period the middle classes had gained so much power (and had successfully converted large enough portions of the upper classes to their cultural ideals) that they were more likely to see the lower classes, not the higher, as their real enemies. More commonly, Doyle's depiction of aristocratic villains discloses fears about their ability to jeopardize the security of the middle classes whose economic and social fate was now bound up with theirs. Elsewhere this fear is figuratively represented as an invasion of the family circle. In this story, we can find such anxieties symbolized by the tunnel that connects the "shabby-genteel" buildings of Saxe-Coburg Square with "fine shops and stately business premises" that abut them in the next street. By quite literally boring from within, John Clay demonstrates the vulnerability of this proud commercial realm and invades the City and Suburban Bank, which symbolizes bourgeois security (1:242–43).

Since it is not labor but the circulation of capital that provides much of the bourgeoisie's wealth, it is appropriate that the money Clay intends to steal has been borrowed to strengthen the resources of the bank (1:247). The middle- or upper-class life-style maintained largely on credit was a staple of Victorian fiction. Insofar as credit operates figuratively as a kind of borrowed reputation, what is at stake in the robbery attempt is not just gold bullion but a kind of corporate—and perhaps even national—honor, since the money has been borrowed from the Bank of France. Holmes's successful capture of Clay breaks up the dangerous liaison between the highest and lowest reaches of society and protects the borrowed money upon which middle-class honor depends. The particular class interests served by his actions are masked, however, by Watson's closing characterization of him as "a benefactor of the race," as well as by Holmes's dismissal of the case as simply one of those "little problems" that have saved him from "ennui" (1:251).

"The Blue Carbuncle" begins by introducing Henry Baker's hat as a clue that points not to "some deadly story," as Watson supposes, but simply to "one of those whimsical little incidents which will happen when you have four million human beings all jostling each other within the space of a few square miles" (BLUE, 1:328). The unprovoked attack on Henry Baker by a group of "roughs" is just the kind of anonymous danger that many feared from city life. By redirecting attention from the attack itself to the "striking and bizarre" problem presented by the hat, Holmes reassures his readers that the detective can distinguish the real dangers of urban existence from its "innocent" (1:328) mental puzzles. By his reading of Henry Baker's moral as well as physical traits from his "battered billycock," he also reassures them that to one armed with a trained eye and an understanding of the laws of human behavior, no individual can remain anonymous for very long or hope to conceal the truth about his moral character. Henry Baker is a more intellectual man than Jabez Wilson and presumably began life in a higher station. At least at one time he exercised the kind of foresight in protecting his property that for the middle class constitutes a sign of virtue: Holmes remarks that Baker's failure to repair his hat-securer reveals "a moral retrogression" on his part (1:331). He proves to have been an unwitting vehicle in the theft of the carbuncle and is thus in effect absolved of any guilty desire for unearned wealth. Nonetheless, his greater abilities do not prevent him from being a similar object of humor: his pompous manner strikes Watson as merely "comical" (1:337) under the circumstances. His sufferings, like the pawnbroker's, represent simply an intriguing "intellectual problem" (1:329) for Holmes to solve, and he, too, disappears from the story as soon as Holmes's curiosity has been satisfied. If anything, the dismissive treatment of the attack upon him suggests that a man with his gifts has only himself to blame for what happens when he so far disgraces himself as to be found drunkenly roaming the city streets at four o'clock on a Christmas morning.

The crime itself reverses the pattern set by "The Red-Headed League," insofar as here the aristocrat is the victim, not the villain. The Countess of Morcar has been betrayed by her own waiting-maid, Catherine Cusack, in collaboration with the hotel attendant Ryder. The intimate knowledge of their employers possessed by body servants gave them dangerous power, which only their honesty and sense of duty prevented them from exploiting. A servant's betrayal was a peculiarly subversive kind of crime, a violation of that innate respect for one's betters that the upper classes relied upon to preserve their property and their privileges. The frequency with which servants and other employees are implicated in crimes in the Holmes canon doubtless mirrored genuine Victorian anxieties that the lower classes were not really as quiescent about the social order as the upper reaches of society would like to think. This is not to say that Holmes is all that solicitous about the countess's loss. As is usual in his adventures, he serves the aristocracy but seldom finds much to admire or respect in them. He reels off the list of lurid crimes the carbuncle has already occasioned, as if to imply that such aristocratic "toys" were more of a social nuisance than the legitimate perquisite of the wealthy, before he rather casually drops the countess a line to let her know the stone is safe (1:335). Describing gems as "the devil's pet baits" characterizes the wrong done as a moral weakness rather than a revolutionary act, and the thief appropriately turns out to be the cringing first-time offender James Ryder. Confronted with such an obvious "shrimp," Holmes is inclined to make light of his wrong as the result of a greed too understandable to be completely condemned: "Well, the temptation of sudden wealth so easily acquired was too much for you, as it has been for better men before you" (1:343). Ryder's attempt to pin the theft on the innocent plumber, John Horner, is more villainous in Holmes's eyes than the desire for the stone itself, and once assured that the other man will not suffer, he lets Ryder go.

The full power of Holmes's unofficial status becomes clear in this tale. He is "not retained by the police to supply their deficiencies," and can thus take the position of one who subverts the law in the name of a higher good—no less than the saving of Ryder's soul. Convinced by the man's terror that he "will not go wrong again," Holmes allows him to escape, lest putting him in jail make a hardened criminal of him (1:346). This story's setting in the "season of forgiveness" (it appeared in the January 1892 issue of the *Strand*) casts Holmes's generosity as an appropriate manifestation of the Christmas spirit. But such forgiveness is easier to muster, given the circumstances, as the contrast with "The Red-Headed League" makes clear: Ryder's very incompetence makes him much less of a threat to society than the cool and calculating James Clay, just as the snatching of a countess's bauble has far fewer repercussions for society at large than an attempt on a bank. In these stories, the proletariat simply does not possess the ability to mount serious threats against the social order. Holmes may appear to stand outside the law on a higher moral ground, but his actions are based on a careful and ultimately comforting calculation of the risks involved for the status quo.

"The Engineer's Thumb" picks up on motifs presented in both of these stories. Here, too, the exorbitant amount of money offered to Victor Hatherly for an hour's work should have made him suspicious, and once again the source of danger is foreign, in the German coiner who masquerades as Colonel Lysander Stark and has entangled the British Dr. Becher as an accomplice. The crime of counterfeiting cuts in several figurative directions in this story. The country estate that should be the seat of the landed gentry proves instead a front for criminal activity, and the men who by their professions should be trusted to uphold respectable values of honor and fair play prove to be either frauds or traitors, "out-and-out pirates who will leave no survivor from a captured ship" (ENGR, 1:384). The magnitude of their wrongdoing also reinforces the view voiced elsewhere that when they do go wrong, higher-class characters (and doctors in particular) make the most dangerous crooks. Counterfeiting also strikes at the heart of the supply and demand that capitalism depends upon by flooding the market with bogus coins that decrease the value of each real one. But in actuality, the counterfeits expose the fiction that money is "real" in any literal sense. The coin is a sign of the immaterial value whose circulation produces wealth in a capitalist economy. The fact that a plausible substitute for that sign can be accepted as having the same exchange value underscores the absence of intrinsic worth in the sign itself and exposes the artificiality of a system that depends upon the acceptance of signs for substances.

Insofar as he agrees to keep the deposit of fuller's earth that Stark has supposedly discovered a secret from the neighbors onto whose lands it extends (1:376), Victor Hatherly collaborates with him to defraud them of the full value of their property and thus participates in Stark and Becher's violation of trust in this story. The shocking violence of his punishment—the cutting off of his thumb—when compared to the embarrassment Jabez Wilson suffers corresponds to the greater seriousness of his crime. The vulgar Wilson and the sniveling Ryder could be expected to respond to the lure of easy money, but as a middle-class professional, Victor Hatherly should have known better than to expect rich rewards for so insignificant an amount of work and significantly earns nothing for his troubles. Then again, at least his personal suffering cannot be dismissed as a mere source of amusement as Wilson's was.

The shadowy figure of Elise, the beautiful German woman who helps him escape death, offers an additional commentary on class issues in this story. Although Doyle may have used her simply to inject a note of romance into what is otherwise a rather thin story line, she also plays a role typical of the genteel Victorian lady that her rich dress denotes (1:378). The middle-class woman was supposed to be the guardian of those moral and emotional values that the brutal marketplace denied and to offer her menfolk a safe haven in which their better selves could be reconstituted in retreat from the dehumanizing effects of the public world. Elise first appears holding a lamp that illuminates the darkness of the old house, just as she lightens the moral darkness of the plot by acting as Hatherly's "saviour" (1:383). In urging him to leave the house before it is too late, she is warning him away from the literal dangers that befell the last hydraulic engineer, but she is also figuratively warning him against sacrificing his well-being for mere money. Hatherly stubbornly resists her assertion that "it is not worth your while to wait" (1:379), refusing to abandon his fee on the word of a woman who might, for all he knew, be mentally unbalanced (a plausible suspicion where women in the Holmes stories are concerned, as we shall see in chapter 9). The fact that he is injured when, instead of saving himself, he chivalrously hangs back in order to make sure that she is not ill used by her companions for helping him (1:383) suggests symbolically that he has learned his lesson and now acknowledges the gender roles proper to middle-class life, including the validity of her attempt to recall him to his better self. In the end, she apparently acts as his guardian angel once again, helping to transport him to safety after he loses consciousness.

Stephen Knight offered a related interpretation of this story that links it and "The Man with the Twisted Lip" to Doyle's personal conflicts about his own career and self-respect at the time. Noting that "The Engineer's Thumb" falls in the second series of stories that Doyle wrote for the *Strand*, a series that Doyle initially resisted writing, feeling that such popular work distracted him from more worthy literary endeavors, Knight pointed to the similarities between Hatherly and Doyle at the time. Those long, lonely hours Hatherly passes in his office, waiting for customers who never show up, bear a striking resemblance to Doyle's lack of early success in his medical practice (M&A, 89–90). Both men are financially unsuccessful at being "consulting scientific specialists" and are "seduced by a lucrative offer that turns out to be disabling." Knight also identified similarities in the appearances of Stark and Becher and those of Greenhough Smith and George Newnes, respectively the editor and proprietor of the *Strand*, the men who in effect bribed Doyle to keep supplying more Holmes adventures. Physical similarities also linked the young Doyle and Hatherly, whose lost thumb represents a symbolic castration as the price paid for selling out as he does. The burned house offers a partial revenge to Doyle/Hatherly, although the villains have vanished rather than being destroyed. Holmes's almost complete passivity in this story underscores its irresolution about the personal issues it has raised, and both Doyle and Hatherly are left at its conclusion with their ability to fashion stories from their experiences as their only lasting gain from this adventure (Knight, 100–101).

In these three stories, individuals who succumb to the lure of easy wealth fail to achieve their ends and are to different degrees punished for their desires. The next four to be discussed involve cases in which individuals have in some sense succeeded in profiting from disreputable sources but the concealment of the truth generates criminal situations that wind up jeopardizing the innocent. Their plots are driven by the importance of respectable appearances and the infection of dishonesty that the attempt to maintain them often breeds.

GUILTY SECRETS: "THE BOSCOMBE VALLEY MYSTERY," "THE FIVE ORANGE PIPS," "THE MAN WITH THE TWISTED LIP," AND "THE BERYL CORONET"

The British Empire, particularly England's vast colonial holdings in India, Australia, and Africa, provided a tremendous source of national wealth during the nineteenth century, much of it gained in more or less exploitative ways. It also offered individuals many shady opportunities for getting rich quick, free from the solicitous eye of the policeman who was always within hailing distance back home in law-abiding England (BOSC, 1:287). What could not be challenged directly on a national level, where colonial wealth was applauded as aggrandizing national honor, could on the individual level be interrogated as a source of guilt. In "The Boscombe Valley Mystery," however, we find that the origins of wealth are judged less blameworthy than the attempt to conceal them. It is because John Turner, who back in the Australian colonies was none other than the notorious Black Jack of Ballarat, attempts to masquerade in England as a respectable Herefordshire gentleman that he becomes vulnerable to blackmail at the hands of Charles McCarthy. As we should expect in a society in which wealth is so important, one of the first clues Holmes picks up on is the fact that despite their obvious differences in wealth, Turner and McCarthy live "upon terms of perfect equality" (BOSC, 1:269); Turner's gratuitous kindness to one who "appears to have so little [money] of his own" is inherently suspicious (1:280). Even though Turner's generosity turns out to be motivated by guilt, his murderous revenge on McCarthy becomes excusable in part because he is shown to possess the behavioral instincts of a gentleman and McCarthy does not. He and his gang had shot the troopers defending the gold shipment without compunction, but he at least restrained himself from killing McCarthy, who as the wagon driver was in a sense an unarmed and innocent bystander. The sting is drawn from Turner's outlaw past by the fact that he tried to atone for it by settling down to "a quiet and respectable life" and doing some unspecified kind of good to make up for the way in which he had earned his wealth (1:287).

Turner's daughter Alice plays an important role in his rehabilitation, but also in instigating his crime. His desire to make himself worthy of her respect signifies his willingness to accept the uplifting function that gentility assigned to woman: from her earliest infancy, her "baby wee hand seemed to lead [him] down the right path" (1:287). Ironically, the cost of this respect is the concealment of his true past, and McCarthy takes advantage of the fact that Turner is more afraid of her knowing the truth than he is of the police. The vulgar McCarthy, whose "wicked little eyes" (1:287) and disreputable taste for horse racing (and doubtless the gambling that went with it; 1:269) suggest his inferiority to the dignified, reserved Turner, confirms his unworthiness by his ungentlemanly attitude toward Alice. Viewing her as merely a source of wealth and not a moral prize, he finally provokes Turner's murderous anger when he urges his son to marry Alice "with as little regard for what she might think as if she were a slut from off the streets" (1:288).

By admitting that he has no right to judge Turner and letting him escape punishment, Holmes in effect approves of Turner's chivalrous defense of his daughter's honor against McCarthy's "foul tongue" and judges McCarthy's contemptible stooping to blackmail as a more blameworthy offense than Turner's career of armed robbery. Turner, after all, earned his wealth openly, if illicitly, and has been successfully rehabilitated into genteel respectability. He has become morally worthy of his economic position in a way that McCarthy, who covertly enriches himself by preying on another's reputation, never can. Holmes collaborates with Turner to allow James McCarthy to be tried as the murderer and to conceal from Alice the truth about her father's past, and eventually makes it possible for the two young people to enjoy Turner's wealth in ignorance of its true origins. As Priestman suggested, it is as if ill-gained riches from foreign plunder are somehow justified as the reward of the enterprising spirit that won them in the first place, even if they must be transferred into "the redeeming hands of a new generation" to be fully tolerable (80).

Holmes casts this case in the same moral terms that he will use at the end of "The Blue Carbuncle." Once again he feels no compunction to correct the deficiencies of the police. Having supplied Lestrade with a description of the murderer, his conscience is free to act outside the law in order to serve the ends of a higher justice. He attributes Turner's downfall to a "temptation" to which anyone—even himself—might succumb and laments the fact that "fate" plays such tricks on "poor, helpless worms." He is content to leave the man "to answer for [his] deed at a higher court than the Assizes" (1:288–89). Doyle's formulation of the issues here works to mystify the economic facts of middle-class life in several ways. We are in effect asked to endorse the belief that the middle class's genteel behavior justifies its possession of wealth and position and not to inquire too deeply into the origin of either. McCarthy's parasitic attempt to enrich himself without working is implicitly treated as more reprehensible than Turner's out-and-out robbery, when in fact both depend on a profiting from the labor of others that is central to capitalism. We are expected to condemn McCarthy's insulting attitude toward Alice Turner as unworthy of a gentleman, despite the fact that middle-class marriages were often motivated by the wealth an heiress would provide her husband, who usually assumed control of it. As was often the case in Victorian fiction, the successful economic exchange that the impending marriage of James McCarthy and Alice Turner represents is concealed under the rhetoric of true love and living happily ever after (1:289). The story's ending guides us away from examining the economic issues involved, by persuading us that Holmes acts on the higher grounds of what is morally and romantically the right thing to do.

Before leaving "Boscombe Valley," let us also note that Turner's is not the only guilty secret fueling this plot. James McCarthy's clandestine marriage to a Bristol barmaid frustrates his father's plans for him to marry Alice and prevents him from being able to clear his own name. Although Turner hates the thought of having McCarthy "blood" mixed with his own, James demonstrates by his behavior that (unlike his father) he is at least potentially worthy of the genteel station that a marriage with Alice would provide, which helps explain why Holmes does nothing to further her father's opposition to their union. Holmes immediately recognizes that James's "frank acceptance" of his arrest was, under the circumstances, a sign of his innocence, not of his guilt. His obvious lack of self-interest or inventive imagination in defending himself (1:271, 275) is the clearest sign of that "manly" openness of character prized by the middle class, which preferred to believe that its social position was freely awarded for its obvious superiority of character and not the result of any vulgar social climbing or calculated maneuvering to advance its own interests. James may have so far forgotten his duty as to raise his voice (and his hand) against his father, but at least shows a "healthy" self-reproach and contrition later (1:272). Besides, given that we accept this same "foul" tongue-lashing by the elder McCarthy as an understandable provocation for his murder by Turner, we can hardly judge the son more harshly. The support of Alice Turner, cast in the role of the genteel woman-as-savior for him as well as for her father, is also a powerful testimony to his worthiness.

As for James's secret marriage to a lower-class woman, there are several reasons why it should not bar his future rehabilitation into a genteel marriage with Alice. The idealization of middle-class Victorian women as pure, chaste, and innocent moral guides implied that they were without sexual desires of their own. Alice's concern to protect James justifies her temporary loss of the "natural reserve" (1:275) such a woman should normally feel in publically defending an eligible young man. She presents their relationship as that of siblings, not lovers, and indicates her genuine romantic attachment to James only by the "quick blush" that quickly passes over her face (1:276). With women of his own class understandably off limits, where else would the young man turn to indulge his natural sexual appetites but to working-class women who were not saddled with an ideology of sexual purity? His Bristol barmaid is portrayed as the real sexual predator in this case. She turns out to be a bigamist who, not content with one husband already in the Bermuda Dockyards, has inveigled the presumably passive and compliant James into her "clutches" and (unlike the loyal Alice) drops him as soon as she finds out he is in trouble (1:279). In light of the fact that many young middle-class men in James's circumstances would simply have kept a working-class mistress, he is to be commended for at least accepting marriage as the cost of his sexual indulgence. Of course, nothing less would have been possible, given the family audience of the *Strand*; it was one thing for the father to know full well that boys would be boys and must sow their sexual wild oats, but quite another to have it acknowledged to his wife and (female) children in print. But here, too, James's very failure to act in an exploitative and self-interested way is another sign that he possesses the innate respectability and honesty that will eventually justify his marriage to Alice, even if he is made to suffer for his earlier sexual indulgence. Holmes tacitly acts to support the double standard in sexual conduct by helping James to conceal his shameful first marriage and by allowing Alice to continue to believe that it was solely James's chivalrous desire not to expose her own name to public scrutiny that prevented him from telling the coroner the full circumstances of his argument with his father shortly before the murder (1:276). Once again, Holmes helps to preserve the security of the middle-class family by protecting its secrets and, in the process, guaranteeing that its wealth will stay within the family.

"The Five Orange Pips" is another story in which a scandalous foreign past threatens an innocent heir. James Openshaw unfortunately finds that he has inherited his uncle's curse along with his wealth. The exact significance of this curse needs some teasing out. It seems that it is not the racism of the Ku Klux Klan that is really blameworthy but the secret society's terrorism against those who did not agree with it. Colonel Elias Openshaw's service in the Confederate Army is not presented as shameful: "He had done his duty well and had borne the repute of a brave soldier" (FIVE, 1:295). Nor is his opposition to carpetbaggers and the enfranchisement of blacks specifically targeted as criminal. Presumably many southerners shared his views on race. What "the better classes of the community" objected to in the Klan was its anonymous campaign of intimidation and assassination against "those who were opposed to its views" (FIVE, 1:302), particularly, we can assume, when its victims were white. As with Moriarty's crime network, the frightening power of the Klan comes from its "perfect. . . organization" and "systematic. . . methods" (1:302); it turns the entrepreneurial skills that gave the middle class much of its economic power to the criminal end of forcing others to foreswear what they believe to be right. Without secrecy, it cannot survive, and so the organization collapses after the defection of Colonel Openshaw with the incriminating papers.

We never really know whether the colonel takes the papers simply to protect himself from their revenge or to break up the society; are the "sins" he describes as overtaking him when the pips arrive (1:293) his participation in the Klan in the first place or his attempt to abscond with its papers and thus to subvert its goals? (That he is guilty of something is clear to Holmes from the very fact of his desire for privacy; 1:301). In any case, his fellow Klansmen view him as threatening because he is in a position to blackmail "some of the first men in the South" (1:303). That is, like Charles McCarthy he has the ability to bring scandal and criminal prosecution down on guilty men who assume a respectable position in society. They murder him to revenge themselves for his betrayal of the Klan's aims, but they must get the papers back to protect their reputations. It is also not clear why Colonel Openshaw believes he will "checkmate" them by destroying the papers that represent his most potent defensive weapon before his attackers arrive (1:293), since they do not know this and, as a result, continue to pursue his family. Perhaps his drunkenness, violent temper, and foul mouth (1:292) are supposed to suggest a culpable lack of foresight and moral strength on his part. He lacks John Turner's and Neville St. Clair's concern to shield his heirs from the damage that results from his own wrongdoing. Or perhaps, following Moretti, we can argue that withholding secrets of any kind is an inherently punishable act and that Josiah Openshaw's refusal to reveal the truth of his past life to his brother and nephew condemns them to the same fate he suffers.

This is another story in which Holmes plays a notably passive role. Insofar as he counsels James Openshaw to leave the remaining incriminating paper on the sundial as directed and to write that the others had been destroyed, he does not really oppose the attempts of the Klan members to protect their guilty reputations. Although he intends to let the law punish them, once they have hurt his pride by snatching James Openshaw out from under his protection his revenge becomes personal and he acts as "[his] own police" (1:304). He thus again serves in his usual unofficial role of protecting prominent members of society from scandal and enabling private forms of revenge to take their course. (Interestingly, James has come to him on the advice of a Major Prendergast, whom Holmes saved from being wrongfully accused of cheating at cards; 1:291.) Although the young man is only first-generation gentry—like many Victorian manufacturers, his father made enough money in industry "to retire upon a handsome competence" and pursue the life of the leisure class (1:292)—his innate air of refinement and delicacy demonstrates that he is worthy of the station he finds himself in. It is a sign of the enormity of the evil represented by the Klan that it strikes down so innocent and so eligible a member of society.

American readers are of course less likely than Doyle's original audience to mistake the letters KKK for the initials of some frighteningly powerful person and perhaps find the author's attempt to infuse the mystery with a kind of Gothic intensity (complete with the stereotypical "dark and stormy night" atmospherics) to be rather strained. By exaggerating the evil it represents—its members are characterized as devils (1:294, 304), and James feels himself paralyzed "in the grasp of some resistless, inexorable evil, which no foresight and no precautions can guard against" (1:297)—Doyle aggrandizes Holmes's ability to banish Gothic terrors with energy and rational common sense. He rallies the terrified young heir ("'Tut! Tut!' cried Sherlock Holmes. 'You must act, man, or you are lost'") and uses his encyclopedia to reveal the supernaturally powerful force as simply another manifestation of the "miserable ways of our fellowmen" (1:303). The fact that the wrongdoers foil his attempts to protect Openshaw and escape, requiring a kind of divine retribution (in the shape of a storm at sea) finally to punish them, however, does suggest that ultimately this case is morally out of Holmes's hands. Although Holmes usually solves the mysteries surrounding secret societies and pacts, he is often too late to avert the deaths they instigate, the murders in *A Study in Scarlet* and *The Sign of Four* being cases in point. I am inclined to agree with Martin Priestman, who argued that if there is a message in these failures, it is "that these alien activities are no concern of British justice, though they are of God," as indicated by the violent weather that often accompanies the evil-doing (Priestman, 79). Holmes is most efficient when acting on the home front to resolve cases of domestic disorder; exotic foreign conflicts are usually simply expelled from orderly England or adjudicated by a higher source of justice.

"The Man with the Twisted Lip" is a much more disturbing meditation on the costs of protecting middle-class reputation because here the danger cannot be externalized. The mystery surrounding Neville St. Clair arouses anxieties that its solution cannot completely lay to rest. The story winds up interrogating assumptions about social identity central to the project of Holmesian detection: it exposes contradictions between the source of wealth and the respectability it buys and raises doubts about the reality of the innate differences in character that were supposedly readable from external social appearances. Neville St. Clair was able on the strength of the money he "appeared" to possess to set himself up in a tasteful villa in Lee and marry into the local bourgeoisie. He had "no occupation," as befits a gentleman, but traveled to town most days to pursue some unspecified business interests (TWIS, 1:312). The very vagueness of his background raises disquieting issues about middle-class identity. He was readily accepted from the outset as a gentleman, presumably on the basis of that air of refinement we later find him to possess, and it is simply assumed that his wealth comes from a respectable source. As Audrey Jaffe pointed out in her penetrating analysis of this story, the fact that the Victorian gentleman was by definition distanced from direct labor meant that the exact source of his wealth was never quite visible. All too often, Victorian financial smashes revealed that prominent reputations had been founded on money that was in fact nonexistent.[2] Nor were the exact circumstances that allowed the gentleman to obtain wealth so easily examined. The successful deception that St. Clair has carried off for years—using money earned in a disreputable way to support a genteel life-style—was made possible by the very ease with which the appearance of wealth was taken to represent the reality of middle-class respectability.

The fact that St. Clair becomes rich while posing as a beggar plays off other anxieties about labor and wealth in a capitalist society. It speaks to the popular rags-to-riches romance in which a beggar could actually become a gentleman through luck or hard work, but also hints at its opposite, the reduction of the gentleman to the pauper at the hands of fate, in the guise of uncontrollable market forces. In either case, the possibility of reversal tacitly undermines the intrinsic distinction between such social positions that the detective story seeks to maintain (A. Jaffe, 97). So, too, does the issue of whether St. Clair is a "real" beggar or not. Begging violated police regulations, and so "Hugh Boone" had to pretend to sell matches instead. But neither the public nor the police is really fooled by this fiction. The money that "rains" down on him is not exchanged for merchandise, but is rather "charity" given because he is "a piteous spectacle" (TWIS, 1:315). Crippled and deformed, he is assumed to be incapable of earning his living through active labor, and his counterfeiting of his disability violates public trust as well as the law of exchange that underlies it in this case. The rising tide of urban poverty in later nineteenth-century London had increased anxiety about maintaining the distinction between the morally "worthy" and "unworthy" poor. Unable to acknowledge the way market forces and population patterns condemned many to under- or unemployment, later Victorians feared that the urban masses were exploiting public charity in order to avoid the necessity of honest labor.[3] Neville St. Clair in effect confirms such fears by admitting that he took up begging when he discovered how much more lucrative it was than the "arduous" work of being a journalist (1:326). The police ultimately insist that "there must be no more of Hugh Boone" (1:327), not only to firm up the boundary between gentleman and beggar but also to validate the distinction between the false beggar and the true one.

As was the case in "Boscombe Valley," what is at stake here is at least in part the ability of the next generation to maintain and profit from the father's privileged social status, despite its disreputable origins. When Holmes chides him for not confiding in his wife (who, presumably, would have recalled him to his better self), St. Clair replies that he had hidden the truth in order to protect his children from embarrassment. In a society in which good reputation was everything, being punished for a murder he did not commit was preferable to admitting the betrayal of respectability that he really was guilty of and thereby saddling his heirs with a crippling family shame (1:325).

Stephen Knight saw in St. Clair's experience another figurative reflection of Doyle's frustration at indulging the public with more Holmes stories (98–99). Both men are writers who are seduced by the lure of wealth into doing something each feels is below him. St. Clair has in effect crippled and deformed himself morally by selling out, by letting the desire for money overrule his pride and stooping to a task far beneath his social station. Suggestively, the makeup that transforms him into the lower-class Boone is likened to dirt that has to be washed off in order to restore him to his clean, middle-class self. The fact that he can so easily be restored to what is represented as his true self surely functions as a kind of reassurance to his creator. Holmes in this case plays his usual role of preserving middle-class prerogatives by concealing gentlemen's secrets. In exchange for a frank confession from St. Clair and his solemn oath as a gentleman (1:327) that he will abandon his deceit, he agrees to keep the truth out of the public court of law. The fervent "God bless you!" that Holmes receives from St. Clair in response (1:325) highlights what we are to believe is the essential moral correctness of this bargain.

The security of St. Clair's gentility is hedged in a number of ways in this story. We have already noted the "refined-looking" appearance and the verbal wit that suggest his inherent class superiority. It is also significant that he first turns seriously to begging in order to cover a debt of honor. He had agreed to lend his name as security for money borrowed by a friend. When the friend defaulted, St. Clair himself was expected to pay off the loan. Rather than default himself, he assumes the fiscal responsibility befitting his class and goes to work to earn the £25 in question (1:325). And notwithstanding the public characterization of begging as an escape from work, his behavior is presented in terms suggestive of bourgeois enterprise. He is, after all, accepted as a "professional" beggar, one who plies a "trade" (1:314) with considerable vigor and success. He not only offers matches in return for the coins tossed to him but entertains passersby with witty comments as well. His skill in exploiting his talents to their best advantage has allowed him to surpass his competitors; in fact, it has made him "a recognized character in the City" (the separately incorporated part of London traditionally associated with business and finance), and thus not so very different from the successful entrepreneur that his pose as the "well-dressed man about town" suggests (1:326). He prudently saves his money and invests it in a country estate and communicates his tender and protective concern for his wife, even in his worst moments. And like many another gentleman, he finds it painless enough simply to pay off the police for his minor infractions of the law (1:327).

The contrast with the pathetic Isa Whitney, whom Watson must fetch home from the opium den at the story's start, is illuminating. A hopeless addict, Whitney offers an even more serious warning than does St. Clair of the damage incurred by the gentleman who loses his self-respect and self-control. Although both men are in a sense victims, Whitney turns out to be a spineless sot who has betrayed his respectable position in society by giving himself over to self-indulgent "orgies" (1:307) during which he completely forgets about his long-suffering wife. Notwithstanding his superior social assets (he has a college education and an illustrious brother, while St. Clair is a schoolmaster's son who has had to make his own way in life), he lacks precisely the will and force of character that have made St. Clair a successful entrepreneur who turns out to be the lascar's employer rather than his victim. We should also weigh the emphatic difference between Whitney's opium use and Holmes's indulgence in cocaine. The latter is characterized not as an escape from responsibility but as a relief from boredom necessary to protect the detective's extraordinary intellectual abilities. Holmes's apparent idleness, like Hugh Boone's, is tacitly less blameworthy because it turns out to be a means to a productive end.[4]

All in all, we are given no reason to doubt that Neville St. Clair is innately worthy of the genteel status to which he returns at the end of the story. Still, the story has revealed a fluidity in social identity that the final restoration of class boundaries cannot entirely contain. Apparently, St. Clair's voluntary consent to these boundaries is not quite enough. Inspector Bradstreet must threaten exposure, should he attempt to escape once again from the identity that the police have determined is appropriate for him (1:327). Surveillance is still needed in a society in which appearances can be deceiving and the middle class can misuse its superior talents to subvert social and economic categories. The city still makes possible an anonymity that nourishes secret selves; the opium den stands discreetly ready to accommodate those who would destroy others or themselves. Although we are glad to have Holmes on the job, his relative marginality in this plot suggests that the order he defends is less under his control and less self-policing than we would like to believe.

I have chosen to end this chapter with "The Beryl Coronet" because it combines several previously discussed motifs—the aristocratic criminal, the question of reputation in a credit economy, and the family scandal, for instance—but also looks forward to issues of gender that will be highlighted in chapter 9. The tragedy that nearly engulfs Alexander Holder is a matter of both "public disgrace" and "private affliction" (BERY, 1:409) in which the dangerous instability of female sexuality plays a key role. The main villain of the piece is Sir George Burnwell, a type of the "unregenerate aristocrat postulated by a long melodramatic tradition as the chief enemy of bourgeois order" (Priestman, 84). In addition to stealing the coronet, he has corrupted Holder's son Arthur, leading him to adopt the wasteful and irresponsible habits of the aristocratic rake, and has seduced his adoptive daughter, Mary. Nonetheless, Holder himself bears some responsibility for his family's vulnerability to such influences, having spoiled his son and misjudged his daughter, in both cases for rather selfish reasons.

His suffering stems at least in part from his inability properly to recognize and support genteel values. Holder's wealth and prominence as "the senior partner in the second largest private banking concern in the City of London" is not enough to guarantee his gentility. The aristocracy and gentry, who could afford to live off the income from their property, had traditionally looked down on those who earned their money directly through business and industry as vulgar. Although the power of commercial wealth to ensure social acceptance had increased during the nineteenth century, snobbish suspicions lingered that plutocrats lacked "class" in both a real and a metaphorical sense, however respectable they might have become. Aristocrats might be all too willing to exploit bourgeois wealth for their own benefit, but they were far from accepting the donors as their social equals.

These class tensions complicate Holder's relationship to the other shadowy aristocrat in the story. The attempted theft is made possible in the first place because "one of the highest, noblest, most exalted names in England" has left the coronet in security for a loan to cover his personal debts. Several critics have suggested a resemblance between this character and the future Edward VII, who as Prince of Wales was notorious for dissolute behavior during his long wait to assume the English throne, although of course Holder, like Watson, is too discreet to name names. An interesting symbiosis of bourgeois and aristocratic interests can be traced through this situation. As Holder points out, the wealth of his banking house depends not just on cash actually deposited with it but on profits earned from the circulation of money in investments, the "most lucrative" of which is the interest gained from loans to people whose "security is unimpeachable." Chief among these are noble families forced from time to time to offer the "pictures, libraries, or plate" (1:410) that are the inherited symbols of their aristocratic stature as security for the ready cash that the bourgeois financial system can provide. In effect, the bank makes money in exchange for protecting noble reputations; it not only allows the elite to preserve the integrity of their estates but also prevents the public exposure of their financial embarrassments that having to sell their property or borrow from their peers would bring about.

Plotting Social Order

The unnamed nobleman tells Holder that he could of course borrow so "trifling" a sum as £50,000 from his "friends," but prefers to make the loan "a matter of business" in order to avoid placing himself under any "obligations" to people with the social power to use their knowledge against him. He is in effect willing to pay Holder whatever interest the banker feels is justified "to be discreet and to refrain from all gossip on the matter" (1:410). Obviously, the reason why he needs the money is a private and dishonorable one, which makes it all the more outrageous that he offers as security "one of the most precious public possessions of the empire," the Beryl Coronet (1:411). By doing so, he is able, ironically, to turn the tables on Holder. Suddenly it is the banker whose reputation is at issue; the nobleman condescendingly tells him that the deposit of the coronet represents "a strong proof of the confidence which I have in you, founded upon all that I have heard of you." The loan to cover his own private debts escalates into a matter of national interest to which Holder's reputation is hostaged, insofar as he now bears the responsibility for averting "a great public scandal" by protecting the security of the coronet (and also, by extension, keeping secret the noble's need for money and his imprudence in pawning the coronet to get it). "Overwhelmed by the honour" of handling the nobleman's business, the banker allows the aristocrat to overbear his doubts about the matter (1:410–11).

Holder takes the coronet home, trusting to the private space of the family to be safer than the public space of an office, only to find that middle-class sanctum vulnerable to a combination of internal betrayal and external invasion (Priestman, 84). Let me reiterate that Holder's inability to judge his own children is in part at fault for the tragedy here. Given that gambling debts most plausibly explain the noble's pressing need for a short-term loan, it is doubly ironic that Arthur Holder's request for money to cover his own gaming debts is what activates his father's suspicions against him. Holder is obsequiously willing to overlook—for that matter, to facilitate—the noble's reckless attempts to conceal his irresponsibility, while condemning his own son for having the honesty to admit his need for money to those closest to him. Having been denied by his father, presumably Arthur will be forced to turn to public moneylenders, who are hardly likely to be so tender of his reputation as his father was of the nobleman's. If we are inclined to blame Arthur for violating middle-class ideals of prudence and thrift by getting into debt in the first place, we must admit that he had tried repeatedly to "break away from the dangerous company he was keeping," only to be drawn back in against his will by the fascinating Sir George Burnwell (1:413). Doyle's middle-class readers would have been all too ready to credit the stock situation in which dissipated aristocrats cynically traded acceptance by their fashionable clubs for the opportunity of bleeding heirs to middle-class fortunes at their gaming tables.

For all his weaknesses, Arthur turns out to have the true instincts of gentility that his "charming manners" (1:412) hint at. When Holmes lectures Holder at the end of the story for not recognizing his son's nobility of character, he points to Arthur's chivalrous desire to protect his cousin's reputation as a trait that should make any gentleman proud of his son (1:425). After having actually prevented the theft of the coronet, Arthur allows himself to be arrested as the suspected thief rather than expose Mary to public scandal as an accomplice in the crime. We have seen a version of this behavior before in James McCarthy, who incriminated himself by refusing to divulge that Alice Turner was the source of his disagreement with his father. Like James's, Arthur's very refusal to invent alibis to defend himself offers strong proof to Holmes of his honesty, and in both stories, the genteel woman vouches for the innocence of the suspect. This kind of respect and protection for women's reputations is of course an important indicator of gentle values. The aristocrats in this story are markedly ignoble in their treatment of women: the Prince of Wales was notorious for his mistresses and Sir George Burnwell has seduced "a hundred" women before Mary with vows of love (1:425). The fact that she is judged not fully worthy of Arthur's solicitude (1:426) actually makes his willingness to sacrifice himself for the sake of a principle—protecting the woman he loves from disgrace—more creditable to him. Like the nameless nobleman who exploits his father's rectitude in order to protect himself, Burnwell also uses Arthur's sense of honor against him, counting on his not being able to reveal the baronet's guilt "without compromising his own family" (1:428).

Holder's misjudgment of Mary is the real source of vulnerability in this household, but their relationship raises some complicated issues about female behavior, the further development of which will have to wait until chapter 9. Mary in many respects fulfills the domestic ideal of the middle-class woman. Holder describes her as a "sunbeam" in his house, "sweet, loving, beautiful, a wonderful manager and housekeeper, yet as tender and quiet and gentle as a woman could be." She is his "right hand," in a very real sense a substitute for his dead wife (1:413). Holder's blindness to her true character arises largely out of a selfish complacency on his part. He simply assumes that playing the self-sacrificing "angel in the house" (to quote a famous Victorian poem sequence idealizing woman's role) satisfies her as much as it does him. Most seriously, he denies that she has any romantic desires of her own. He fully expected her dutifully to marry Arthur and to draw him back to the straight and narrow (1:413). After she disappoints him by refusing his son's hand, he takes it for granted that she wishes for no company but his and shares his suspicions about Burnwell's character. By describing her as "not so very young" at 24, he avoids acknowledging that his "little Mary" is still of an age when she might expect to find emotional gratification outside the family circle. Like the other stepfathers who try to prevent their daughters from marrying in order to monopolize their assets for their own benefit in *The Adventures of Sherlock Holmes*, Holder can be seen as exerting "quasi-incestuous pressures" (Priestman, 84) on Mary, and not the least of Burnwell's attractions may have been the escape from this claustrophobic family circle that he appeared to offer her.

We should not doubt that Mary loves her adoptive "dad" or that her "sweet womanly caress" and her concern for Arthur's well-being are genuine (1:419). Regrettably, however, she is one of those "women in whom the love of a lover extinguishes all other loves" (1:425). Although we may find Holder's insensitivity to her needs blameworthy, Mary puts herself beyond the pale of middle-class female respectability by actively pursuing those sexual desires that the

Victorian ideal of woman worked so hard to deny. She in effect acknowledges this by writing herself off as one lost to decent society in the farewell note she leaves her uncle, which begs him not to search for her and proclaims her rather ominously to be his loving Mary "in life or in death" (1:424). Her voluntary abandonment of respectable society helps explain why Holmes at the story's end rather callously leaves her to suffering and disgrace at the hands of Sir George Burnwell, who, as any man of the world would realize, has no intention of marrying her. For the middle-class woman, sexual indulgence brings its own punishment.

Class differences in sexual mores are subtly underscored in this story by the treatment of the maid Lucy Parr. Holder predictably finds her attractiveness to men a "drawback" in her employment (1:412), an implicit threat to the security of the household, even though he believes her to be "good"—that is, chaste. Mary exploits this anxiety by attempting to transfer suspicion to the maid. When Holder finds his niece at the hall window, Mary tells him that Lucy as been out to "see someone" at the side gate and that this "is hardly safe and should be stopped" (1:414). The middle class views the regulation of servant sexuality as a form of self-protection. Lucy deserves to have no romantic secrets, so of course Holmes infers that there "could be no possible reason" to suspect that Arthur was lying to protect her (1:428). As is frequently the case, the emotional life of the working classes is here treated as being more comic than dangerous, and Lucy's suspicious tryst turns out to be nothing more than an "escapade with her wooden-legged lover" (1:426). The middle-class woman's indulgence of sexual desire is much more subversive of social order, however, and thus nothing short of ostracism from polite society is possible for Mary.

Holmes allows Sir George Burnwell to escape without prosecution because he knows that there is no way to punish the baronet without a scandal, one that would presumably expose Mary's sins as well as the nobleman's imprudence in pawning the coronet. Thus, we find Holmes in his usual position of protecting the power of the middle and upper classes by protecting their secrets, even when that means subverting the law. But why does Holmes apparently pocket £1,000 as "a little reward" for himself in this case (1:424)? Although he hardly condones the behavior of the corrupt aristocrats in the story, it seems that the genteel Holmes is, like them, not above profiting from a wealthy financier, especially one who, like Holder, needs to be taught a lesson. Holmes distracts attention from his own gain in the case by lecturing Holder on the debt of apology he owes to his son, whose true nobility Holder could not recognize (1:425). Although the father cannot rise above his business interests to value his son rightly, Arthur's self-sacrificing sense of honor suggests that Holder's wealth will be satisfactorily joined with true gentility in the next generation, the same kind of promise that ends "The Boscombe Valley Mystery."

In addition to their lively plotting and entertaining characterization, *The Adventures of Sherlock Holmes* offer readers implicitly contradictory reassurances. They create a fantasy of scientific predictability and control while still insisting on the efficacy and value of individual effort (Knight, 75). The pervasive determinism assumed to structure human behavior in Holmesian detection does not absolve individuals of the responsibility for the moral decisions they make or take anything away from the merits of acting honorably. Treating true gentility as a condition that must be in some sense earned ultimately strengthens its value and conceals the economic determinants of this society. In these tales the possession of money, property, and landed estates does not guarantee that their owners are fully worthy of the social status that comes with them. This must be demonstrated by appropriate kinds of principled actions and respect for class ideals. Holmes agrees to conceal the secrets of the McCarthy, Turner, Openshaw, and Holder families because the next generation shows by their behavior that they are morally worthy of the wealth and position they will inherit. The implication, in other words, is that the laws of England are being bent not to serve the interests of a particular class but to ensure that a higher moral code will prevail. The selective applications of justice that Holmes is responsible for never really threaten social order because it is assumed that the signs of genuine merit cannot be counterfeited, so that wealth and power will eventually fall into the hands of those best able to exercise them. Like much detective fiction, the Sherlock Holmes stories draw their ideological effectiveness from this ability to conceal the unconscious political choices they make under the guise of a socially neutral higher justice that in practice, however, always winds up favoring the interests of a particular class. We may no longer identify with this class in the way that Doyle's contemporary readers would have done, but we still yearn for his reassurance that in the world of Sherlock Holmes at least, the guilty cannot prosper indefinitely and the truly worthy will eventually find their just reward.

9

"Cherchez la femme"

In the end, it all boils down to sex and money; these, in varying mixtures, are the chief motivators of crime in the Holmes canon, as in detective fiction in general. I have chosen my chapter title, French for "seek the woman," to focus attention on assumptions about the problematic nature of female sexuality in such texts. The fact that this phrase has long outlived its source, Alexandre Dumas's detective novel *The Mohicans of Paris* (1854–55), and entered into common parlance suggests the extent to which our society still assumes that women are somehow more directly responsible for the disruptions caused by sexual desire than are men. This may be in part an acknowledgment that in a world in which power has conventionally been controlled by males, women are viewed as having no real agency, except as sexual irritants or distractions. Whenever the smooth progress of male order is derailed, we suspect that sexual desire has caused the obstruction and look for the woman who inspired it. In the process, the blame for disorder is shifted away from male desire to the female who arouses it, so that her sexuality becomes dangerous in a way his does not. Consider the original source of this phrase. Regardless of whether he was investigating abduction, burglary, sacrilege, or suicide, the universal response of the police detective Monsieur Jackal was first to "seek the woman." Although his conviction that every crime could be linked to a female is treated as a faintly comic "monomania" on the part of this eccentric character, the narrator assures us that it always succeeded in leading him to the criminal. The specific example Jackal gives, in which he solved the death of a tiler by determining that he had lost his footing on the roof while peeping at a woman getting dressed, seems a particularly telling case of blaming the victim. By arguing that men are puppets whose wires are pulled by women, Jackal in effect holds women responsible for aberrant and destructive male desires.[1]

While more suave about the ways of the world than the lower-middle-class Jackal, Sherlock Holmes usually shares in his assumptions about the connections between women and crime. He tells Watson, for instance, that had there been women in Jabez Wilson's household (that is, sexually desirable women, since the 14-year-old servant girl apparently does not count), he would first have suspected "a mere vulgar intrigue" as the motive for getting the pawnbroker out of the house (REDH, 1:250). Most often, however, he focuses on the more general emotional vulnerability that sexual desire creates. As an observer, he considers "the softer passions" admirable for "drawing the veil from men's motives and actions" but scrupulously excludes all romantic desires from his own life, lest they interfere with his reasoning processes. Significantly, Irene Adler remains "the" woman in his life not for her physical charms but because she has outsmarted him (SCAN, 1:209).

Sexual desire is the most powerful threat to the ideal of rational order and self-control championed by the middle classes in Victorian society. "Crimes of passion," which are always on some level crimes involving sexual passion, are treated as less blameworthy than those calculated in cold blood because in the former we assume that emotion has overwhelmed reason and morality. But the appropriate regulation of the libido constituted the middle classes' most important qualification for social power, so that passion rendered them socially as well as emotionally vulnerable. In the Holmes stories, uncontrolled emotions inspire the eccentricity that is always somehow culpable in the bourgeois world. To take a minor comic example, think about the Dundas divorce case mentioned at the beginning of "A Case of Identity," in which the husband ends each meal by hurling his false teeth at his wife (1:252). Sexual irregularity is the chief factor in scandal, the most frequent cause of those "delicate" situations that demand Holmes's skill in shielding reputations. The elaborate strictures that Victorians placed upon sexual conduct paid tribute to the disruptive potency that sexuality was feared to possess. In particular, the ideal of the pure, self-sacrificing, and essentially asexual Victorian lady served to channel the most volatile form of sexuality—the feminine—into socially stabilizing forms.

The Holmes stories reinforce the widely shared assumption that women present graver threats to sexual stability than do men. Mary Holder's fate in "The Beryl Coronet" shows us how severely the genteel woman is punished when she allows sexual desire to override the domestic loyalties that were her chief duty in life. She is held responsible for undermining middle-class values, but she is also in a sense punished for challenging male control of female sexuality, in the form of her uncle's assumption that she could (should?) have no desires beyond the family circle. Such an overthrow of accepted order can only lead to crime, the plot implies. And although we are on Elise's side in "The Engineer's Thumb," it is also the case that her defiance of male control effectively breaks up the counterfeiting operation in Berkshire. An independent income can also allow women to escape male subordination and is also portrayed as criminally tempting to others (usually men). Doyle demonstrates this most pointedly in "The Disappearance of Lady Frances Carfax." There Holmes describes the "drifting and friendless woman" as "one of the most dangerous classes in the world," for the wealth that gives her mobility is also "the inevitable inciter of crime in others" when she forsakes male protection (LADY, 2:401). The independent incomes to which Mary Sutherland, the Stoner twins, and Alice Rucastle can lay claim are also what attract their (step)fathers' malevolence in the *Adventures* that we shall shortly consider.

A more subtle form of male control over female sexuality is suggested by the middle- and upper-class woman's particular vulnerability to blackmail. Whereas Holmes (at least initially) dismisses Irene

Adler's threat to blackmail the King of Bohemia as insignificant, he takes Charles Augustus Milverton's attempts quite seriously in the story that bears his name, precisely because Milverton's victims are portrayed mainly as women who cannot fight back without destroying their own reputations. The susceptibility of such ladies to "genteel ruffians" who gain their affections and then betray their secrets reiterates the criminal danger that inheres in women's attempts to act on their desires outside the channels approved by their male guardians (CHAR, 1:792). But this imbalance of power also has an economic dimension. The Victorian lady can be blackmailed for even her most innocent romantic dalliances because her virginity is essential to her value in the marriage exchange; the mere hint of compromised emotions damages her chances of making a good match. Holmes is called in when Milverton threatens to send Lady Eva Blackwell's fiancé some letters she wrote to another man before her engagement. The fact that her former love was an "impecunious squire" and her fiancé is the Earl of Dovercourt is important here. Although the letters are merely "imprudent" in Holmes' terms and "sprightly" in Milverton's, both know that the earl, in lowering himself to marry a lady distinguished more by her beauty than by her wealth, expects the most extreme sort of chastity from Lady Eva and would break off the match should he learn that she had earlier expressed romantic interest in another man, especially one so far beneath him socially. And Milverton expects that rather than allow her to lose so eligible a husband, Lady Eva's friends and relatives will be willing to lend her money to meet his ransom demands (CHAR, 1:793–94). In "The Second Stain," Lady Hilda Trelawny Hope similarly becomes the victim of a blackmailer because of an "indiscreet" letter written before her marriage. Despite her characterization of it as merely a "foolish" note written by "an impulsive, loving girl," she fears that evidence of her previous romantic attachment would be considered "criminal"—that it would, in effect, raise questions about her premarital chastity—in the eyes of her straitlaced husband, the secretary for European affairs (SECO, 1:921).

We should acknowledge that Holmes himself is no prude where such matters are concerned. His sympathy for the plight of Lady Eva and of Lady Hilda (as well as for Philip Green, the lover whose wild youth had led the fanatically pure Lady Frances Carfax to refuse him her hand, despite her continuing love for him; LADY, 2:407) implicitly lays the blame for their dilemmas on the too exacting sexual mores of Victorian society. This attitude (as well as the love triangles that so frequently motivate his plots in the later stories) may well represent a deflection of conflicts that Doyle himself felt. No matter how scrupulously chaste they kept their relationship, his secret love for Jean Leckie while still married to his first wife would still have been strongly condemned by a wide segment of society at the time. Doyle was sufficiently sensitive to issues of sexual conduct to delay the publication in book form of "The Cardboard Box" for more than 15 years because its plot turned on adultery (although this is indicated by nothing more risqué than the woman going for a pleasure boat ride with another man in her husband's absence).[2] But so long as the woman in question was pure of heart (and did not compromise herself physically) her conduct was not condemned.

This broadmindedness about romantic love can distract attention from more problematic aspects of female nature as portrayed in the Holmes canon. Holmes's attitudes toward women may have a comic edge because of his inveterate misogyny. Only the most heartless intellect could cut short Mary Morstan's tearful account of her father's disappearance with a curt request for dates and details (SIGN, 1:115), and surely we are meant to second Watson's view that it is "atrocious" of Holmes to claim that the best of women could not be trusted, even if we take the doctor's trust with a grain of salt because he is smitten by Miss Morstan, the woman in question (SIGN, 1:163). But most of Holmes's generalizations about women fit too well with the rationalistic enterprise presented in the rest of the canon for us to judge them too skeptically. The actions of female characters almost always confirm the stereotypes Holmes presents: women are naturally secretive (SCAN, 1:223), pertinacious, and cunning (REDC, 2:341), or have a greater capacity for anger when wronged (ILLU, 2:471). Women are allowed their female intuition, of course (BOSC, 1:276; TWIS, 1:320), but this is the kind of skill always conceded to primitive, untutored intellects; it is no real match for logic and reasoning. The purported regularity of women's behavior toward men plays an important role in constructing "the world of ideal conformity which, perhaps, it is one of the subliminal aims of detective fiction to create" (Priestman, 91). Holmes's deductions about Henry Baker in "The Blue Carbuncle" depend on the assumption that all loving wives brush their husbands' hats, for instance. Elsewhere Holmes elaborates an implausibly specific set of rules for interpreting female behavior: "When a woman thinks that her house is on fire, her instinct is at once to rush to the thing which she values most" (SCAN, 1:226). A woman's "oscillation upon the pavement always means an *affaire de coeur* [an affair of the heart]," but if she has been seriously wronged the "usual symptom" would be a doorbell broken in indignation (IDEN, 1:253). When a woman is agitated, she might "fly to her tea" (CROO, 1:571) but would never send a reply-paid telegram (WIST, 2:294). No properly devoted wife would allow a servant to prevent her from viewing her husband's mangled body (VALL, 2:196).

The common thread in these examples seems to be the assumption that women in general (like the lower classes in Holmes stories) have less rational control over their emotions: their behavior, like medical "symptoms," cannot be suppressed. But this point also supports Holmes's somewhat contradictory complaint that women's actions frustrate investigation because they are too *un*predictable—at least according to male standards. "The motives of women are so inscrutable," Holmes muses in "The Second Stain." "Their most trivial action may mean volumes, or their most extraordinary conduct may depend upon a hairpin or a curling tongs." A man might avoid sitting in the light in order to conceal his guilty expression from Holmes's keen scrutiny, but a woman might do so simply because her nose was unpowdered (SECO, 1:912). Although there is an underlying stereotype at work here—that woman's natural vanity overrules her reason—it is also the case that fickle females create a gap in the project of total interpretability that the Holmesian project of detection promises to deliver. Catherine Belsey found a similar kind of gap in these texts' reticence about the "shadowy, mysterious and often silent women" who motivate their plots. Although Holmes's methods purport to reveal even the most bizarre mysteries as susceptible to rational explanation, these tales cannot be explicit about exactly what women like Lady Eva (or Milverton's unnamed murderer and former victim) has done or written without undermining our sympathy for them. Indeed, Lady Eva never even appears in the story. As a result, their sexual experiences remain in some sense beyond the reach of the rationality that claims to know and understand everything in human behavior.[3]

It is also the case that notwithstanding Holmes's generalizations about female nature, all women are not created equal in these stories and that class and ethnicity predict significant differences among them. The jealousy that is axiomatic in female nature is intensified by the foreign, often "tropical" blood that fills the veins of wronged wives and mistresses, especially in later stories like "The Sussex Vampire" and "Thor Bridge." Englishwomen, particularly those of the higher classes, exercise more control over their bodies and their secrets. Working-class women are doubly marked for exploitation in these stories: the same class conventions that make their bodies available for sexual consumption by gentlemen govern the taking of information as well. Holmes's "peculiarly ingratiating way with women" (GOLD, 1:854), his "almost hypnotic power of soothing" them (REDC, 2:341), is shown to be particularly effective in inducing lower-class women to reveal what he wants to know (see, for example, the way he "thawed" Lady Brackenstall's chilly maid in "The Abbey Grange," 1:893). Naturally, he chides Watson for not being similarly resourceful in obtaining evidence in "The Retired Colourman": "What about the girl at the post-office, or the wife of the greengrocer? I can picture you whispering soft nothings with the young lady at the Blue Anchor, and receiving hard somethings in exchange" (2:654). Holmes relies on this same convenient confusion between sexual and factual exchange in "Charles Augustus Milverton," when he courts and even becomes engaged to Milverton's housemaid (another of Belsey's invisible women) in order to gain information about her master's house and habits. Gentlewomen, like gentlemen, have more success in resisting the detective's intrusion into their motives. Lady Hilda uses disguise to subvert the police in "The Second Stain," and Lady Brackenstall's charming personality at least temporarily deceives Holmes in "The Abbey Grange." The coldly reserved Violet de Merville positively infuriates the detective by resisting his arguments against her fiancé, the evil Baron Gruner, in "The Illustrious Client" (2:475).

When gender is an issue in the Holmes stories, it invariably enters in the form of a woman whose relationship to typically feminine roles or behavior is the source of disorder. Finally, though, the construction of woman's "nature" cannot be isolated from the web of issues that captures class, wealth, and reputation in a network of social power. These stories work to contain the threat of disruption by ultimately reinforcing gender role boundaries, but the way those boundaries are drawn has much to do with the woman's economic and social identity. I have organized the following exploration of these issues by grouping stories that feature similar power dynamics. All involve situations in which the security of ostensibly more powerful males is jeopardized by the resistance of women to their desires. In the first two, high-society marriages create situations in which socially less powerful women can endanger the wealth and/or reputation of elite males. The last three explore the troubling problematics of patriarchal power in Victorian society by imagining the kinds of violence unleashed by fathers who try to usurp their daughters' fortunes and, at least symbolically, their sexual freedom.

MARRIAGES OF CONVENIENCE: "A SCANDAL IN BOHEMIA" AND "THE NOBLE BACHELOR"

We become aware of the complicated interweaving of passion and power almost from the outset of "A Scandal in Bohemia." The King of Bohemia's position bears striking similarities to that of the unnamed aristocrat who sets in motion the near disaster of "The Beryl Coronet." Like him, the king's disreputable secret life has made him vulnerable to scandal, and he handles his case in person to avoid giving anyone else dangerous power over him (1:215). Like the anonymous nobleman, the king shifts attention away from his personal failings by casting the problem in the light of a national emergency—a matter "of such weight it may have an influence upon European history" (1:214).

Marriages among royalty were formed primarily to consolidate wealth and power, not to satisfy emotional or sexual needs. Indeed, we may well pity the king for the chilly embraces he will have to endure from his strictly proper Scandinavian princess as the cost of affiliating his royal family with hers, although his obscure comment about secrecy no longer mattering after two years (1:214) may imply that he has little intention of continuing to toe the line once he and his royal bride have been inextricably wedded. Holmes never questions whether this goal justifies the suppression of truth necessary to obtain it. Dallying with mistresses is clearly a monarch's prerogative; not just the double standard but his immensely greater social power is on the king's side, and so Holmes knows that he could get away with simply denying the authenticity of any written documents. But photographs have a problematic facticity that renders such lies useless. Holmes, however, is quite ready to turn burglar in order to remove this last obstacle to the king's tactically important marriage.

Irene Adler's dubious social position is of course a critical factor here. Had she been some victimized gentlewoman, the king's actions would doubtless have been viewed somewhat differently. But she fits the stock character of the "adventuress," as the king calls her—not quite a prostitute, but definitely not respectable—who exploited sexual liaisons at high levels of society for her own financial benefit. In an era that made the suppression of sexuality and self-display the price of female respectability, the public careers of actresses, singers, and dancers were considered almost by definition to connote sexual promiscuity. The expression "a young person of the theater" (echoed by Holmes's initial reference to Irene as a "young person"; 1:215) was a euphemism for a prostitute, and the Irene Adler character suggests parallels to such famous nineteenth-century actress-courtesans as Lola Montez, who had an affair with Louis of Bavaria during Doyle's youth, and Lillie Langtry, the Prince of Wales's most famous mistress.[4] And yet Irene's character is not quite that easy to pigeonhole. To begin with, she is no ordinary chorus girl but an artist talented enough to have sung at such major European opera houses as La Scala and the Imperial Opera of Warsaw. The king refers to her as "the well-known adventuress, Irene Adler," and yet she is clearly no household name to

Holmes, who must look her up in his index. Although she resides in St. John's Wood, a suburb favored by Victorian men for keeping their mistresses, the neighborhood grooms whom Holmes pumps for information would hardly be so admiring of a woman whom they considered merely a gold-digging harlot (C. Redmond, 71). Most important, her actions refute the idea that her main concern is money. Not only does she refuse to sell the photograph, but she is finally content to marry a modestly situated London lawyer.

Despite her questionable reputation, Irene is actually more closely in line with middle-class values than is the king, and this does much to tip the balance of readers' sympathies. Her description of herself as "cruelly wronged" by him (1:229), as well as his conviction that she would do anything to prevent him from marrying another woman (1:216–17) or that she could not really love Godfrey Norton (1:227), imply some genuine love on her part that he has callously betrayed by abandoning her for a more lucrative match—or worse, by taking it for granted that she would be willing to continue their liaison, despite his impending marriage. In either case, the king winds up in the position of one who cynically marries solely for personal gain, while Irene, like the idealized gentlewoman, marries solely for love. He breaks his vows, but "her word is inviolate" (1:229). The showy vulgarity of his dress (1:213) mirrors his coarser sensibilities, while her dainty beauty is the appropriate counterpart of her finer sense of honor and values. No wonder Holmes agrees (with a sarcasm lost on the king) that Irene does indeed occupy "a very different level" from His Majesty (1:229). Once again, a callous aristocrat shows himself to be the moral inferior of those motivated by middle-class ideals. Irene also satisfies traditional womanly roles by her tender concern for the supposedly injured Holmes, disguised as a clergyman. Her generosity is enough to shame the ever-susceptible Watson, but he decides that solidarity with Holmes must override chivalry in this case, and hardens his heart against her (1:225). Men, after all, must stick together to contain the dangerous power of women.

It is true that a fair amount of evasion is necessary to maintain our sympathies for Irene. There are a number of unanswered questions in the story. What exactly are Irene and the king depicted as doing in the incriminating photograph? (More knowing readers would be aware of the flourishing trade in pornographic pictures and might suspect something more racy than a simple joint portrait). Does Godfrey Norton know the full details of her relationship with the king or not? Has he seen the photo, or does Irene keep it (as she claims) to prevent the king from using it to blackmail her? Was she Norton's mistress before she was his wife, and if so, what accounts for their haste in marrying? What would they have done had Holmes not entered the fray when he did? Belsey's argument about "Charles Augustus Milverton" (110–11) is also relevant here: silence about the exact nature of Irene and the king's conduct prevents the reader from having to confront contradictions inherent in the ideological assumptions the story makes. We are simultaneously able to believe Irene to be the king's superior in terms of character and not to question the essential justice of Holmes's willingness to break the law in order to protect the monarch's interests. We can sympathize with her as a wronged woman but still endorse the status quo.

Perhaps most important to maintaining this balance is Irene's demonstration that she possesses the internalized self-control and self-respect that were so important to middle-class power. She seriously threatens male authority. Her very social marginality increases the damage she could do to the king's reputation. Notwithstanding her stereotypically female response to fire, for instance, masculine traits like a "soul of steel" and "the mind of the most resolute of men" (1:216) give her the courage and skill to turn the tables not just on the two-timing monarch but on Holmes as well. Her usurpation of male dress allows her to enjoy male freedoms, like roaming the London streets alone, and her escape with the incriminating photograph is a direct revenge on Holmes for manipulating her into revealing what he wanted to know (1:228). The potential subversiveness of her powers is blunted, however, by her willingness to hold her hand and rise above petty revenge. Domesticated love, woman's true vocation, leads her to submit in the end to voluntary exile as a devoted wife. Rather than challenging the power structure, she ultimately serves the same ends as Holmes by allowing the upper classes to escape social and legal reprisals for their wrongdoing.

Lord Robert St. Simon is not so lucky as the King of Bohemia, even if he is somewhat less culpable. Their situations are similar in a number of ways. As usual, Holmes is called in as one who has been recommended for his utmost "discretion" in handling delicate—that is, sexually embarrassing—affairs for the aristocracy and nobility. Lord Robert's aristocratic "friends" have been unsuccessful in hushing up the matter of his bride's disappearance, and he engages Holmes more to quiet the scandal swirling around his name than out of concern for what has happened to Hatty Doran. He turns out to be another aristocrat whose snobbish assurance of his own social preeminence is implicitly criticized by his clear lack of any true nobility of spirit.

Lord Robert exploits the same double standard as the King of Bohemia in forwarding his plans for a lucrative marriage. An aging fop, he has clearly not spent his adult life saving himself for the right woman, and chances are that he would not be curtailing his sexual freedom now if it were not for his family's financial needs. It is "an open secret" that his father, the duke, has been so pressed for money as to sell off the Balmoral art collection, an important symbol of the family's aristocratic prestige. In any case, as a younger son, Lord Robert must look elsewhere for wealth. Despite the coy comments of the society columnists about American heiresses invading and conquering noble British houses, they quite clearly recognize that the real predators are impoverished aristocrats ready enough to snap up social nobodies with six-figure dowries (NOBL, 1:391), and it is at best disingenuous of Lord Robert to pretend that such sums are too commonplace in his family for him to have paid much attention to Hatty's fortune (1:395). Like the King of Bohemia, Lord Robert fears that a former mistress, angry at being spurned, may jeopardize his profitable match. Flora Millar is quite unequivocally "a young person of the theater"; lest there be any doubt of this, the newspaper euphemism *danseuse* (French for female dancer) conjures up the titillating undress of the French music hall in the Gay Nineties (NOBL, 1:393). Flora has followed the *danseuse*'s typical career and left the theater to be kept as a gentleman's mistress. But where their long and *"very"* friendly"—that is, sexually intimate—relationship has apparently been based on some genuine devotion on her part, Lord Robert sees it purely in financial terms and feels that having paid generously for his pleasure, he now owes Flora nothing else (1:397). Coming shortly after this admission, his surmise that Hatty might be overwhelmed by the "immense social stride" she had made in marrying him (1:398) rings particularly hollow.

If Irene Adler's disreputable side reappears, somewhat debased, in Flora Millar, her honorable traits are also magnified in the more thoroughly respectable Hatty Doran. Hatty, like Irene, is an American, which according to contemporary stereotypes in part explains and somewhat excuses their greater sexual freedom. A child of the Wild West, Hatty lacks Irene's elegance but demonstrates the same redeeming fidelity to her true love. Hatty too poses subtle challenges to male authority by her rejection of female stereotypes. She is a slangy tomboy "unfettered by any sort of traditions," who "ran free in a mining camp" in her youth and defied her father's wishes by continuing to see and then secretly to marry Frank Moulton (1:395, 403). No demure self-effacement for this "wild" and "impetuous" woman who shares Irene's resolution and courage in acting upon her decisions. But the danger that her "volcanic" (1:395) emotions will seriously disrupt masculine order is once again blunted by her voluntary subordination to feminine ideals. She has defied her father, it is true, but only because she (unlike St. Simon) wished to marry for love, not for money. Similarly, she does not think twice about deserting the more prestigious lord once she knows Frank is still alive; indeed, she could do nothing else without soon dishonoring herself as a bigamist or an adulterer. Her unconventional departure from the wedding breakfast is excused by her not having a mother alive to counsel her on such delicate matters (1:402) and ultimately serves the conventional end of transferring her (and presumably her fortune) to the authority of her true husband. Notwithstanding some gaucheness on their part, Hatty's openness and warmth and Frank's forthright desire to reveal the truth at all costs make them more morally admirable characters than the cold, selfish, and hypocritically snobbish Lord Robert. Moreover, their upright behavior signifies that they are more intrinsically worthy to possess great wealth than is he, so that there is a certain justice in leaving their two fortunes (for Frank, too, has become rich enough to stay at the best hotels) in American hands, rather than allowing a parasitic and degenerate English aristocrat to profit from the money. In the final analysis, though, Holmes rather cynically reaffirms the status quo, much as he tacitly does in "A Scandal in Bohemia." Not only does he raise no objection to Lord Robert's callous pursuit of a rich wife, but he actively sympathizes with him, calling on Watson to be merciful to a man whose ungracious behavior is quite understandable given his loss of wife and fortune after he had worked so hard to earn both (1:407). We are apparently supposed to admire people (especially women) who marry for love, but not to begrudge those (especially men) who follow good business sense in making their feelings pay off in what was, after all, a common strategy for social advancement during the period.

FAMILY AFFAIRS: "A CASE OF IDENTITY," "THE SPECKLED BAND," AND "THE COPPER BEECHES"

The pattern that emerged in chapter 8 is reinforced in those stories focusing on women and sexuality—the tendency of the *Adventures* to avoid challenging the institutional or social bases of power by implying that the reform of individuals, and not structures, is all that is needed to correct society's problems. Our father-daughter triad will offer no exception to this rule. Although the first two stories offer us the spectacle of the evil stepfather, as if to distinguish between the truly loving father and the unscrupulous outsider who exploits those in his trust (Moretti, 140), "The Copper Beeches" suggests that there is no real difference between the two. None of these tales questions the principle of patriarchal power over daughters or can imagine a lady allowed to enjoy her own wealth outside the control of the father or his surrogate, her husband.

James Windibank's closeness in age to his stepdaughter, Mary Sutherland, and his successful masquerade as her suitor throw into the highest relief the entanglement of sexual and financial power over women and make most explicit the symbolically incestuous pressures

116

brought to bear by fathers seeking to prevent their daughters from becoming the possession of other men in all three stories. In the other two, the girl's mother is dead and cannot protect her. In "A Case of Identity," the mother abets her husband's plot against her own daughter, loudly admiring the "passion" shown by Hosmer Angel toward Mary and encouraging their early marriage (IDEN, 1:257). What do we make of such a mother? Are we supposed to think her typical of the older woman who must be subservient to every demand (especially financial) of her much younger husband in order to keep him, or are Windibank's attractions such that he can manipulate her as easily as he does her daughter? This is another case in which, by remaining mute about the full motives (sexual and otherwise) of a woman significant to the plot but missing from the action, the narrative can avoid examining ideological contradictions, such as that between parental love and economic self-interest.

Ultimately it is Windibank's social unworthiness, and not his desire to control his stepdaughter's money, that is treated as most blameworthy in this story, insofar as little is done to disturb the latter arrangement at the story's end. He has underlying economic motives for making Mary's mother sell out her interest in the family plumbing business (so that he can profit from the ready cash) and for trying to prevent Mary from attending social functions with their old circle of friends (so that she will not be tempted by possible suitors), but we are also given no reason to doubt the role snobbery plays in these demands. He considers his position as traveling wine salesman to be "very superior" (1:254) to that of a plumber (presumably because it did not require dirty physical labor) and wants both women to sever all ties, financial and social, to this more vulgar stratum of society. His priggish regret that Mary has washed the family linen in public by consulting Holmes (1:263) echoes the concern with public reputation that gentlefolk are supposed to feel, but in his case we later realize that it is his own exposure, and not his family's privacy, that he really fears for. Windibank demonstrates that he lacks the internalized sense of honor required for true gentility by his legal quibbling when finally exposed by Holmes. The fact that his behavior is not legally "actionable" does nothing to mitigate his gross violation of decency and trust. By labeling his cruel deception "more creditable to his head than to his heart" (1:265), Holmes makes clear that superior intelligence alone is not sufficient to justify one's pretensions to a higher social stature. Appropriately enough, he threatens Windibank with a beating, traditionally the gentleman's extralegal revenge on cads for slights against their sisters and daughters (1:266). Upstarts like Windibank are finally no real threat to the social system because their insensitivity to genteel codes of ethics exposes them as unworthy of real power.

Mary, in much the same way as Irene and Hatty, manifests traits designed to throw Windibank's moral shabbiness into higher relief. Like several characters we have already considered, she demonstrates that she is a worthy conduit for colonial wealth by her modesty and self-respect. She knows and accepts her position in society. She has none of Windibank's shame about her honest, working-class roots and continues to work for a living (at typewriting, one of the new white-collar trades opening up to middle-class women in the late nineteenth century), despite her comfortable inheritance from money made by her uncle Ned in New Zealand. Rather than using her legacy to play the lady of leisure, traveling and indulging herself, and because she has no wish to be a burden at home, she generously contributes the entire sum to her mother and stepfather (1:255). She is dutiful in fulfilling appropriate female roles. An essentially forthright person who hates to "do anything on the sly," she shows proper filial respect by sending a letter asking her stepfather's leave to marry Hosmer Angel (1:257). And her "simple faith" and loyalty to the man she loves, even after he has disappeared, endows her with a nobility of character that her vacuous face and vulgar dress seem to belie (1:259).

Given Windibank's contemptible character and Holmes's obvious sympathy for Mary's plight, it is all the more troubling that the detective in effect does nothing to undercut the father's power at the end of the story. He not only allows Windibank to go free, despite his conviction that the scoundrel's intelligence will allow him to "rise from crime to crime until he. . . ends on a gallows" (1:266), but he does nothing to enlighten Mary about her stepfather's character. Although we can detect the ulterior motives behind Windibank's comments on woman's nature—that there was "no use denying anything to a woman, for she would have her way" (1:256) or that Mary was an "excitable, impulsive girl," not easily controlled when her mind was made up (1:263)—Holmes tacitly seconds them at the end of the story: he will tell her nothing because of the proverbial danger that inheres in snatching delusions (especially romantic ones) from a woman (1:267). Holmes is in effect a collaborator with patriarchal power, one who always considers it "just as well to do business with the male relatives" (1:262) rather than involving irrational women in decisions about their own fate. In the end, he leaves Mary and her money in the continued control of her stepfather. Although Mary Sutherland is much more clearly an innocent victim, her situation bears interesting parallels to that of Mary Holder. Both are in a sense driven into the arms of unsuitable suitors by foster fathers who have their own selfish reasons for expecting the women under their control to "be happy" in their "own family circle" (IDEN, 1:256). Both deceive the men they call father by pursuing a secret lover, and we can consider both to be punished in the end for acting on their own desires. In the world of detection, knowledge is power; Mary Sutherland's continued ignorance promotes the continued exploitation of her wealth and her freedom by her family. The fact that she can be so treated, despite her obvious innocence, provides a veiled reminder of the reprisals that await women who try to escape the bounds set by patriarchal authority, no matter how understandably.

In "The Speckled Band" we find the father-daughter contest transposed into a much more somber key and painted in the heightened colors of the Gothic thriller. Helen and Julia Stoner are purely innocent and ignorant victims of a larger-than-life villain, helpless and abused maidens imprisoned in a gloomy, decaying mansion, threatened by strange beasts and sinister gypsies, in need not just of a detective, but of one who "can see deeply into the manifold wickedness of the human heart" (SPEC 1:349). Here the stepdaughter is conveniently doubled, so that one twin can die the mysterious midnight death demanded by the Gothic plot, while the other can be saved for the happy marriage she so justly deserves. With melodramatic insistence, the stepfather's evil is overdetermined by a piling up of contributing causes: he is not merely greedy but insane, the last link in a degenerate aristocratic family, suffering from a hereditary "violence of temper approaching to mania" that has been further intensified by many years in the feverish tropics. Colossal strength and size are thrown in for good measure (1:350). Sherlock Holmes plays much the same role in this melodrama that he will in the later *Hound of the Baskervilles*, another tale in which terrors verging on the supernatural are ultimately reduced to the work of quite real, if exotic, animals. As the agent of scientific reason and modern justice, Holmes cuts mystery and horror down to size, revealing the usual sordid economic motives at their heart and ensuring that the rightful heirs will be able to enjoy their property.

Jasmine Yong Hall and others noted that the implicitly incestuous pressures that stepfathers bring to bear on stepdaughters are in this story suggested by the imagery of the snake attack as a kind of rape; after "piercing" the wall of Helen's bedroom (1:354), Roylott has her sleep in a bed bolted to the floor so that she cannot escape his snake when it crawls through the hole in the ceiling.[5] Notwithstanding their importance in motivating crime, however, the sisters function as little more than props in this story, where the real contest is once again between the detective and the "male relative," Roylott. On one level, this contest is conducted in the same phallic imagery: Holmes straightens out the poker bent by Roylott and thrashes the doctor's snake with his own bamboo cane (Hall, 300–301), thus proving himself to be the stronger man. But their opposition is figured in class terms as well. Grimesby Roylott is on one level a degenerate aristocrat, traditional enemy to middle-class prerogatives. His violent behavior is the sign of a hereditary weakness as well as a manifestation of the feudal indifference to the rights of others, including his own stepdaughters. His denunciation of Holmes as "the Scotland Yard Jack-in-office" (1:356) is the aristocrat's typical put-down of middle-class workers as vulgar and officious drudges and is of course considered particularly insolent because it denies Holmes his status as a gentleman amateur. But Roylott has also adopted the middle-class lesson of enterprise and self-help. Realizing that, given his family's dwindling fortunes, he "must adapt himself to the new conditions" or waste away as an "aristocratic pauper" (1:349), he obtained a medical degree and went out to the colonies to earn his fortune. There, by virtue of "his professional skill and force of character," he succeeded in establishing a large practice, although he cannot keep it up because of his disorderly conduct. Holmes never denies his intellectual power. Indeed, it is precisely his professional status that makes Roylott so dangerous: "When a doctor does go wrong he is the first of criminals. He has nerve and he has knowledge" (1:364). Nothing is so destabilizing to social order, this implies, as the professional who uses the very skills that afford him status to betray his most sacred responsibilities. Having abandoned his respectable profession to return to Stoke Moran and play the squire on his wife's money, Roylott draws on his formidable mental resources to plot diabolical murders when that income is threatened by his stepdaughters' marriages. Perhaps it is because of his dangerous corruption of both aristocratic and middle-class ideals that Roylott must die, the only criminal in the *Adventures* whom we see meet such an end. Such an outsized melodrama villain cannot finally be contained by the law, and he finds his death in a sensational revenge, as the snake he has trained turns on him (with a little encouragement from Sherlock Holmes).

Holmes reestablishes social order not only by helping to eliminate the evil stepfather but also by ensuring that Helen Stoner and her independent income are confided to the care of her new husband, notwithstanding Mr. Armitage's failure to take seriously the threats against her earlier (1:349). And despite Roylott's egregious criminality, Holmes and Watson play their typical role of suppressing scandal against prominent families. They take care to conceal their true identities from the coachman who drives them to Stoke Moran (1:358) and suppress the truth about Roylott's death until after Helen's death, revealing it then only to squelch rumors that attributed even greater villainy to him (1:346). Unworthy aristocrats and corrupt professionals are self-defeating, the story implies, and the technicalities of the law (such as testifying truthfully about the full circumstances of mysterious deaths) should be bent occasionally in order to protect the reputation and position of the innocent.

"The Copper Beeches" also borrows Gothic motifs: the lonely, stained country house with a mysterious third-floor wing, a damsel imprisoned against her will with the collaboration of disreputable servants, a hint of congenital cruelty in father and son, a wife with a secret sorrow, a monstrous dog patrolling the grounds. As Holmes explains in a later story, he deduces the "criminal habits" of the apparently "smug and respectable father" from the behavior of Rucastle's son (CREE, 2:588), but the first signs of disorder are the ones we have already learned to suspect from stories like "The Red-Headed League": exorbitant payment for eccentric activity. Violet Hunter herself finds the offer of £100 a year for supervising a single child "almost too good to be true," and Holmes concurs that Rucastle must have some ulterior motive (COPP, 1:433, 436). Notwithstanding the lip service paid to the importance of "the bearing and deportment of a lady" in her society, Violet knows that it is not customary to be reimbursed so handsomely simply for possessing such intangible assets. Being "faddy" (COPP, 1:434) in asking Miss Hunter to dress and act in a certain way is also a suspicious sign, although Rucastle presumably tries to make these desires more understandable by attributing them to his wife, on the assumption that "ladies' fancies" are notoriously capricious (1:434). Violet takes this one step further by speculating that the wife is a lunatic (1:436). Looking at their offer from a business point of view, however, she concludes that if they were prey to strange fads, at least they were willing to pay well for their eccentricities. Although Holmes continues to grumble that "no sister of his should ever have accepted such a situation" (1:437), the fact of the matter is that unlike Holmes's hypothetical sister, Violet Hunter is a woman on her own with no family to support her and, as such, has no real financial choice but to accept the job.

What sets this story apart from most in the Holmes canon is the extent to which its action is dominated by women. Most of the narrative consists of Violet Hunter's recounting of her experiences. Sherlock Holmes deduces the gist of the mystery, which most readers will already suspect—that Violet has been brought in to impersonate Alice Rucastle—with little effort and no fanfare late in the story, but his presence is irrelevant to Alice's successful escape, which has been effected with the assistance of the servant, Mrs. Toller. Given Rucastle's iniquity in imprisoning his own daughter, we are for once expected to be on the side of the servant who has cheerfully accepted bribes to undermine her master's authority (and who, in effect, can continue to blackmail him, apparently knowing too much about his wrongdoing to be dismissed at the story's end; 1:451–52). Mrs. Toller is a kind of good foster mother who counterbalances the evil one in this story. She helps the victimized Alice find her way to her true love's arms, while the second Mrs. Rucastle (with assistance from her spiteful child) not only marginalizes Alice's power in her family but also collaborates with her husband to deprive Alice of an income and a husband of her own. The stepmother, in turn, is in a sense doubled by Miss Stoper, the manager of Westaway's employment agency, who apparently thinks nothing of the safety or sacrifice of the governesses she places in jobs so long as she earns a tidy commission from their employers (1:435).

Violet Hunter is the chief catalyst of the story's action. Although Watson with characteristic sentimentality worries about her as a "lonely woman" straying into a "strange side-alley of human experience" (1:437), her courage and self-reliance are virtually unprecedented among women in the Holmes canon. Typically, their sexuality marks female characters as passive victims, ignorant accomplices, or conniving malefactors in these tales. The only other women who exercise real agency or intelligence tend to be duplicitous femmes fatales like Irene Adler. Violet, while neat and lively, is explicitly not sexually threatening or coyly manipulative. She possesses the freckled face of the girl next door and loses her "luxuriant" and symbolically erotic chestnut hair early in the story (1:434). She is also strikingly free of any maternal sentiment for her young charge, Edward Rucastle, dismissing him as a "creature" irrelevant to her story early on (1:441). Like her fictional ancestress, plain Jane Eyre, she is uncharacteristically "observant" (1:445) and alert to the odd occurrences in the isolated country house. Although the burning curiosity that fires her investigation of the vacant wing is treated by Mr. Rucastle as a dangerous form of meddling female inquisitiveness (1:446), in exploring the forbidden areas of the house and holding a mirror to her eyes to see the road behind her as she reads, she is simply investigating the case as a good detective would. She, too, is motivated by a "feeling of duty" and the belief that some good might come of her penetrating the mystery, and her only thought once Holmes has identified Alice Rucastle as the target of the plot is that they "lose not an instant in bringing help to this poor creature" (1:445, 448). No wonder Holmes considers her "a quite exceptional woman" who can be trusted to assist him by locking up Mrs. Toller (1:447). Lest she seem to threaten male prerogatives, however, she is deprived of the steely nerves of the male detective and is driven from her exploration of the abandoned wing by "a mad, unreasoning terror." But even here she maintains sufficient presence of mind to lie about what she has seen when confronted with Rucastle's suspiciously coaxing inquiries (1:446). In any case, she shows gracious feminine tact in recognizing the limits of her abilities and submitting the matter to Holmes.

It would seem that, at least figuratively speaking, the price of Violet's masculine intelligence and independence is that she be left a spinster at the end of the story. Notwithstanding Watson's matchmaking hopes, Holmes's admiration of her turns out to be purely intellectual, and she goes off to pursue her career in education with some success. Alice Rucastle, having found that the quiet patience usually prized in women leads in her case only to exploitation and abuse at the hands of her father, is luckily wrested from his grasp by a lover who proves his worthiness to win her hand (and her fortune) by continuing to stand by her, despite her loss of health and beauty (1:451).

A conventional objective of Victorian fiction is the disposal of marriageable heroines at the story's end. The pattern that emerges from these tales suggests that only those women without independent wealth and/or social position are finally left on their own. Whatever threats of scandal are posed by Irene Adler and Hatty Doran are safely contained in their marriages to men chosen for their character, and not for their wealth or status. The genteel heiresses Helen Stoner and Alice Rucastle willingly submit their freedom and their fortune to suitably genteel husbands. Although an undeniably respectable middle-class girl, Violet Hunter is still a penniless orphan who must work for her living. She is granted considerable professional success, but has nothing to barter away in the marriage market and so is effectively closed out of it. Holmes seems strikingly indifferent to the fate of Mary

Sutherland. Because she occupies the lowest social rung of the six, despite her independent income, her romantic desires are simply not taken seriously, and she is left with delusions about Hosmer Angel that will surely cripple her chances of finding marital happiness anytime in the near future. She is simply outside Holmes's most effective sphere of operation, that of the upper middle and genteel classes, where he consistently operates to reinforce a status quo that guarantees the economic and social power of men. Female nature may be uniform in Holmes's eyes, but women's ability to actualize their desires depends upon the social boundaries that encircle them.

Notwithstanding the incidence of more violent forms of passion and revenge in Doyle's later Sherlock Holmes stories, his focus remained largely turned inward on betrayals within marriage and the family, and he continued to link the restoration of order to the internalized discipline of individuals. World War I dramatically changed the public conception of where the gravest threats to society lay, however, and perhaps the weaknesses perceived by some readers in the later Holmes stories derive at least in part from their failure to respond to their audience's deepest fears about civilization (Clausen, 120). Perhaps what those readers really desired in demanding more Holmes was a return to the securities of that earlier Victorian and Edwardian world, and their somewhat ungrateful disappointment at the Holmes they got was a manifestation of their unconscious unease at finding that his reiteration of the old sureties of class, honor, and reason no longer provided credible assurance against the disintegrating forces of modern society—not just the collective madness of the war but the threatening sexuality of the newly emancipated woman, a growing recognition of the disturbing powers of the unconscious, and the disorienting drift toward relativism in science and philosophy.

Much of the undeniable charm of the Holmes stories lies in their assumption of a world in which scientific investigation confirms rather than undermines traditional values, where exotic and violent crimes can be experienced vicariously while never defeating the detective's rational control, where the healthy impulses of the individual—his or, more often, her voluntary submission to social conventions—can be trusted to guarantee the health of the commonwealth. If we are less likely than Doyle's contemporary readers to accept the social relations portrayed in the stories as natural, the quaint but orderly world they depict still speaks to deep desires. Whether we come to these stories for the incomparable style of the Holmes-Watson partnership or for a glimpse of that late Victorian London caught in the amber of Sir Arthur Conan Doyle's imagination, we come away with a satisfying testimony to the power of the intellect to master crime and mystery. The stories reassure us that the intrinsic worth and identity of individuals can be perceived and thus controlled by the trained eye of the detective who helps guarantee that all will eventually find their just deserts. They lift us, at least temporarily, out of moral confusion and conflicting interests and reach for some ground above partisan concerns where we are convinced that the ends of a higher justice will be satisfied. For all their vivid late Victorian immediacy, their most powerful appeal lies in their ability to ally us with what they represent as timeless values and ideals, a goal that is all the more alluring for being so contested by the relativism of our own world. The adventures of Sherlock Holmes will always retain their definitive place in detective fiction because they work their magic with unparalleled wit and assurance, embracing crime, irrationality, and evil, in order ultimately to reassert justice, reason, and right.

Notes and References

Chapter One

1. Pierre Nordon, *Conan Doyle: A Biography* (New York: Holt, Rinehart and Winston, 1967), 265–66, charts the relationship between the publication dates and the chronological setting of the major stories. Hereafter cited in text.

2. Thomas Henry Huxley, "The Method of Zadig," in *Science and Culture, and Other Essays* (New York: Appleton, 1882).

3. For a discussion of the glorification of the scientist in the Holmes tales, see J. K. Van Dover, "The Lens and the Violin: Sherlock Holmes and the Rescue of Science," *Clues* 9, no. 2 (1988): 37–51.

4. Arthur Conan Doyle, *Memories and Adventures: The Autobiography of Sir Arthur Conan Doyle* (London: Hodder and Stoughton, 1924), 14; hereafter cited in text as M&A.

5. Pasquale Accardo, *Diagnosis and Detection: The Medical Iconography of Sherlock Holmes* (Rutherford, N.J.: Fairleigh Dickinson University Press, 1987), 17; hereafter cited in text.

Chapter Two

1. See Stephen Knight, *Form and Ideology in Crime Fiction* (Bloomington: Indiana University Press, 1980), 70, for a discussion of the *Strand* readership; hereafter cited in text.

2. See Walter Klinefelter, *Sherlock Holmes in Portrait and Profile* (New York: Schocken, 1975), 60–61, for a history of visual portrayals of Holmes.

3. For speculation about Gillette's origination of this phrase, see Richard Lancelyn Green, "Introduction," *The Uncollected Sherlock Holmes* (Harmondsworth, Eng.: Penguin, 1983), 82. The Welles radio version, "The Immortal Sherlock Holmes," originally aired on 25 September 1938 as part of the CBS "Mercury Theatre on the Air."

4. See, for instance, Watson's reference to knowledge of Holmes's activity in several cases, "which I merely shared with all the readers of the daily press" (SCAN, 1:210), or his offer to reveal the "full facts" of the Lord St. Simon marriage scandal that had titillated his audience four years before (NOBL, 1:388).

5. Howard Haycraft, *Murder for Pleasure: The Life and Times of the Detective Story* (New York: Biblo and Tannen, 1968), 56.

Chapter Three

1. Quoted in Green, "Introduction," *The Uncollected Sherlock Holmes*, 43.

2. Although Doyle in some places implied that *Lippincott's* had explicitly asked for a sequel to *A Study in Scarlet*, elsewhere he suggested that it was he who decided that the story he had contracted to write for them would feature his sleuth again (see M&A, 72–73, and Green, "Introduction," *The Uncollected Sherlock Holmes*, 49, 274–75, 347). In a letter to the *Lippincott's* agent, Doyle mentions receiving "30 or 40" favorable reviews for what appeared originally as *The Sign of the Four; or, The Problem of the Sholtos* (quoted in Green, 50–51).

3. Quoted in Green, "Introduction," *The Uncollected Sherlock Holmes*, 57.

4. Doyle recalled this incident in a 1921 speech, quoted in Harold Orel, ed., *Arthur Conan Doyle: Interviews and Recollections* (New York: St. Martin's, 1991), 80.

5. For accounts of the contemporary reception of the Holmes stories, see Doyle, M&A, 93–94; Green, "Introduction," *The Uncollected Sherlock Holmes*, 50–51, 54–57, 66–68; Nordon, 232–33; and John Dickson Carr, *The Life of Sir Arthur Conan Doyle* (New York: Harper and Brothers, 1949), 162–65.

6. Cait Murphy, "The Game's Still Afoot" (*Atlantic Monthly* [March 1987], 58–66), offers a useful history of the "Sherlockian" school; see also Nordon, 207–9.

7. For a very helpful review and analysis of Doyle's biographers, see John L. Lellenberg, ed., *The Quest for Sir Arthur Conan Doyle: Thirteen Biographers in Search of a Life* (Carbondale: Southern Illinois University Press, 1987). Doyle's comments on the identification of Holmes with himself can be found in M&A, 94–95; Green reprints "To an Undiscerning Critic" in *The Uncollected Sherlock Holmes*, 162–63.

8. For a consideration of the appeal of detective fiction to intellectuals, see Marjorie Nicholson, "The Professor and the Detective" in *The Art of the Mystery Story*, ed. Howard Haycraft (New York: Simon and Schuster, 1946),

Notes and References

110–27. Dennis Porter expands on her ideas in *The Pursuit of Crime: Art and Ideology in Detective Fiction* (New Haven, Conn.: Yale University Press, 1981), chap. 12; hereafter cited in text.

9. T. S. Eliot, "The Complete Sherlock Holmes Short Stories: A Review," in *The Baker Street Reader: Cornerstone Writings about Sherlock Holmes*, ed. Philip A. Shreffler (Westport, Conn.: Greenwood Press, 1984), 17–19; W. H. Auden, "The Guilty Vicarage," in *Detective Fiction: A Collection of Critical Essays*, ed. Robin Winks (Englewood Cliffs, N.J.: Prentice-Hall, 1980), 15–24, hereafter cited in text; Edmund Wilson, "Who Cares Who Killed Roger Ackroyd?" in *Detective Fiction*, 36, and "Mr. Holmes, They Were the Footprints of a Gigantic Hound," in *The Baker Street Reader*, 34.

10. Early general histories of detective fiction are: Alma E. Murch, *The Development of the Detective Novel* (New York: Greenwood Press, 1968), hereafter cited in text, and Haycraft, *Murder for Pleasure.* See also Ian Ousby, *The Bloodhounds of Heaven: The Detective in English Fiction from Godwin to Doyle* (Cambridge, Mass.: Harvard University Press, 1976), hereafter cited in text.

11. Geraldine Pederson-Krag, "Detective Stories and the Primal Scene," in *The Poetics of Murder: Detective Fiction and Literary Theory*, ed. Glenn W. Most and William W. Stowe (San Diego: Harcourt Brace Jovanovich, 1983), 19.

12. Samuel Rosenberg, *Naked Is the Best Disguise: The Death and Resurrection of Sherlock Holmes* (Indianapolis: Bobbs-Merrill, 1974).

13. Christopher Redmond, *In Bed with Sherlock Holmes: Sexual Elements in Arthur Conan Doyle's Stories of the Great Detective* (Toronto: Simon and Pierre, 1984).

14. See, for instance, Christopher Clausen, "Sherlock Holmes, Order, and the Late Victorian Mind," *Georgia Review* 38 (1984): 106–10, hereafter cited in text; James Kissane and John Kissane, "Sherlock Holmes and the Ritual of Reason," *Nineteenth-Century Fiction* 17 (1963): 353–62; and Frank McConnell, "Detecting Order amid Disorder," *Wilson Quarterly* 11, no. 2 (1987): 172–83, hereafter cited in text.

15. For a good example of a structuralist approach, see Umberto Eco's analysis of the James Bond novels, "Narrative Structures in Fleming," in *The Role of the Reader: Explorations in the Semiotics of Texts* (Bloomington: Indiana University Press, 1984), 144–72. Eco writes more specifically on the Holmes stories in "Horns, Hooves, Insteps: Some Hypotheses on Three Types of Abduction," in *The Sign of Three: Dupin, Holmes, Peirce*, ed. Umberto Eco and Thomas A. Sebeok (Bloomington: Indiana University Press, 1983), 198–220. *The Sign of Three* offers extended examples of semiotic analysis applied to the Holmes stories. Of course, William of Baskerville, the protago-

nist of Eco's novel *The Name of the Rose*, owes an obvious debt to Sherlock Holmes. For narratological treatments of the detective story, see, for instance, Tzvetan Todorov, "The Typology of Detective Fiction," in *The Poetics of Prose*, trans. Richard Howard (Ithaca, N.Y.: Cornell University Press, 1971), 42–52, or Peter Brooks, *Reading for the Plot: Design and Intention in Narrative* (New York: Knopf, 1984), esp. 24–29; both hereafter cited in text.

16. For such approaches, see, for example, Stephen Knight, *Form and Ideology in Crime Fiction*; Porter, *The Pursuit of Crime*; or Martin Priestman, *Detective Fiction and Literature: The Figure on the Carpet* (New York: St. Martin's, 1991), hereafter cited in text.

Chapter Four

1. Roland Barthes, *S/Z*, trans. Richard Miller (New York: Hill and Wang, 1974), 19–20.

2. The detective story's use of Aristotelian elements has been discussed by W. H. Auden, "The Guilty Vicarage," 16, and Dorothy Sayers, "Aristotle on Detective Fiction," 25–34, in Winks, *Detective Fiction*.

3. Relevant here is the feeling of many readers that Agatha Christie had violated the rules of fair play by making the first-person narrator of *The Murder of Roger Ackroyd* the murderer.

4. Quoted in Green, *The Uncollected Sherlock Holmes*, 131.

5. Brooks arggued th rather than being equivalent to *sjužet*, "plot" cuts across the *fabula/sjužet* distinction as the "interpretive activity elicited by the distinction between *sjužet* and *fabula*" (*Reading for the Plot*, 12).

6. Glenn Most, "The Hippocratic Smile," in *The Poetics of Murder*, 346–47; hereafter cited in text.

7. Roger Caillois, "The Detective Novel as Game," in Most and Stowe, *The Poetics of Murder*, 10–11. For examples of such rules, see S. S. Van Dine, "Twenty Rules for Writing Detective Stories," 189–93, or Ronald Knox, "A Detective Story Decalogue," 195–96, both in Haycraft, *The Art of the Mystery Story*; both pieces originally appeared in 1928.

8. See, for instance, Mark Van Doren's preference for the well-defined characters and fanciful plots of the Holmes stories over those typical of the "naturalistic" modern novel, quoted in Shreffler, *Baker Street Reader*, 22, 30.

9. Franco Moretti, *Signs Taken as Wonders: Essays in the Sociology of Literary Form*, trans. Susan Fischer, David Forgacs, and David Miller (London: Verso, 1983), 137; hereafter cited in text.

10. Michael Holquist, "Whodunit and Other Questions," in Most and Stowe, *The Poetics of Murder*, 158–59; Todorov, 44.

11. Martin A. Kayman, *From Bow Street to Baker Street: Mystery,*

Notes and References

Detection, and Narrative (New York: St. Martin's, 1992), 225–26; hereafter cited in text.

Chapter Five

1. John G. Cawelti, *Adventure, Mystery, and Romance: Formula Stories as Art and Popular Culture* (Chicago: University of Chicago Press, 1976), 9–11; hereafter cited in text.

2. See, for example, George Grella, "Murder and Manner: The Formal Detective Novel," in *Dimensions of Detective Fiction*, ed. Larry N. Landrum, Pat Browne, and Ray B. Browne (n.p.: Popular Press, 1976), 37–57.

3. Kenneth Rexroth puts this kind of eccentricity in a historical context in "Never as Odd Again," 41–43, in Shreffler, *The Baker Street Reader*.

4. For discussions of these shifts in attitudes toward crime, see Kayman, 31–60; Ernest Mandel, *Delightful Murder: A Social History of the Crime Story* (London: Pluto Press, 1984), 1–15, hereafter cited in text; Porter, 146–50; and Michel Foucault, *Discipline and Punish: The Birth of the Prison* (New York: Vintage, 1979), hereafter cited in text.

5. Michael Wheeler, *English Fiction of the Victorian Period 1830–1890* (London: Longman, 1985), 15–16.

6. Knight, 34–35; Murch, 64–65, 122–24. See also Porter, 153–54, and Kayman, 107–10, for Dickens's journalistic promotion of the virtues of the metropolitan police.

7. Robert Louis Stevenson, *The Dynamiter: More New Arabian Nights* (London: Longman, Green, 1885), 6.

8. Clive Bloom, "Capitalising on Poe's Detective: The Dollars and Sense of Nineteenth-Century Detective Fiction," in *Nineteenth-Century Suspense: From Poe to Conan Doyle*, ed. Clive Bloom et al. (New York: St. Martin's, 1988), 19–22. See also Knight, 39–44, and Porter, 120–22, on the class ideals suggested by the Dupin/Holmes type of detective.

9. For a fuller discussion of Holmes's decadent attributes, see Paul Barolsky, "The Case of the Domesticated Aesthete," *Virginia Quarterly Review* 60, no. 3 (1984): 438–52.

10. Letter to Ronald Knox, quoted in Green, *The Uncollected Sherlock Holmes*, 131.

Chapter Six

1. Quoted in Orel, *Arthur Conan Doyle: Interviews and Recollections*, 58.

2. For a brief summary of Bell's abilities and their influence on Holmes, see Thomas A. Sebeok and Jean Umiker-Sebeok, "'You Know My Method': A

Juxtaposition of Charles S. Peirce and Sherlock Holmes," in *The Sign of Three*, 30–36. Nordon found the portrait of Bell in Doyle's *Memories and Adventures* "too like Holmes to be true" and argued that it was created after the fact to "strengthen the illusion that Holmes really existed" (214).

3. Scientific theories can be proved false if they fail correctly to predict or account for results, but they can never be proven correct once and for all, since new evidence might always appear that they could not account for. See Karl Popper, *The Logic of Scientific Discovery* (New York: Basic Books, 1959), 40–42.

4. For a summary of Peircean abduction in the Holmes canon, see Thomas A. Sebeok, "One, Two, Three Spells UBERTY (In Lieu of an Introduction)," in *The Sign of Three*, 7–9. Several other essays in this collection also address similarities between Holmesian and Peircean deductions.

5. Marshall McLuhan, "Sherlock Holmes vs. the Bureaucrat," in Shreffler, *The Baker Street Reader*, 39.

6. Peter V. Conroy, "The Importance of Being Watson," in *Critical Essays on Sir Arthur Conan Doyle*, ed. Harold Orel (New York: G. K. Hall, 1992), 48–52; William Stowe, "From Semiotics to Hermeneutics," in Most and Stowe, *The Poetics of Murder*, 368.

7. Massimo A. Bonfantini and Giampaolo Proni, "To Guess or Not to Guess?" in *The Sign of Three*, 127–28; Kissane and Kissane, "Sherlock Holmes and the Ritual of Reason," *Nineteenth-Century Fiction* 7 (1963): 353–62.

Chapter Seven

1. Carlo Ginzberg, "Clues: Morelli, Freud, and Sherlock Holmes," in *The Sign of Three*, 107–9, traces the development and use of fingerprinting during this period; hereafter cited in text.

2. Quoted in Allan Sekula, "The Body and the Archive," *October* 39 (Winter 1986): 27.

3. For considerations of nineteenth-century racial theories, see Stephen Jay Gould, *The Mismeasure of Man* (New York: Norton, 1981), and Nancy Stepan, *The Idea of Race in Science: Great Britain 1800–1960* (Hamden, Conn.: Archon Books, 1982).

4. Quoted in Green, *The Uncollected Sherlock Holmes*, 364.

5. Examples quoted in Sebeok and Sebeok, "`You Know My Method,'" 32–33.

6. This incident is described in Owen Dudley Edwards, *The Quest for Sherlock Holmes: A Biographical Study of Arthur Conan Doyle* (Totowa, N.J.: Barnes and Noble, 1983), 204.

7. Peter Stallybrass and Allon White, *The Politics and Poetics of Transgression* (Ithaca, N.Y.: Cornell University Press, 1986), discuss these phenomena in chaps. 3 and 4.

Notes and References

8. Walter Benjamin, *Charles Baudelaire: A Lyric Poet in the Era of High Capitalism*, trans. Harry Zohn (New York: New Left Books, 1973), 39–43.

9. Tony Bennett, *Popular Fiction: Technology, Ideology, Production, Reading* (London: Routledge, 1990), 214.

10. Oscar Wilde, "Preface," *The Picture of Dorian Gray* (London: Penguin, 1985), 21.

Chapter Eight

1. Other exceptions might be the allusions to the terrorist activities of the Molly Maguires in *The Valley of Fear* and to the Irish civil war in "His Last Bow" (2:445), both written in Doyle's more pessimistic years around World War I.

2. Audrey Jaffe, "Detecting the Beggar: Arthur Conan Doyle, Henry Mayhew, and 'The Man with the Twisted Lip,'" *Representations* 31 (Summer 1990): 98–99; hereafter cited parenthetically as A. Jaffe.

3. See Gareth Stedman Jones, *Outcast London: A Study in the Relationship between Classes in Victorian Society* (1971; repr. New York: Pantheon, 1984), for a discussion of middle-class attitudes and policies toward the urban poor in later Victorian London.

4. Compare Audrey Jaffe's analysis (110), which finds in the similarities between Holmes and Whitney evidence of middle-class anxieties about apparently unproductive labor.

Chapter Nine

1. Alexandre Dumas, *The Mohicans of Paris* (New York: George Munro, 1878), 34; see also chap. 35, "Seek the Woman."

2. This story originally appeared in the *Strand* for January 1893 but was left out of the *Memoirs of Sherlock Holmes*. It finally appeared in the volume *His Last Bow* (1917).

3. Catherine Belsey, *Critical Practice* (London: Methuen, 1980), 109–17; hereafter cited in text.

4. Michael Harrison identified the meaning of "young person of the theater" in "Sherlock Holmes and the King of Bohemia" (147) in *Beyond Baker Street: A Sherlockian Anthology* (Indianapolis: Bobbs-Merrill, 1976). Nordon (235) identified Irene Adler with Lola Montez, and Christopher Redmond suggested Lillie Langtry, in *In Bed with Sherlock Holmes*, 60–61. My discussion of Irene has profited from a number of Redmond's comments.

5. Jasmin Yong Hall, "Ordering the Sensational: Sherlock Holmes and the Female Gothic," *Studies in Short Fiction* 28 (1991): 298.

Selected Bibliography

Primary Sources

Sherlock Holmes Stories (First English Editions)

A Study in Scarlet. London: Ward, Lock, 1888. First Holmes fiction; first published in *Beeton's Christmas Annual,* 1887.

The Sign of Four. London: Spencer Blackett, 1890. Second Holmes fiction, first published in *Lippincott's Magazine,* 1890.

The Adventures of Sherlock Holmes. London: George Newnes, 1892. First 12 short stories, originally serialized in the *Strand Magazine,* July 1891–June 1892.

The Memoirs of Sherlock Holmes. London: George Newnes, 1894. Second series of short stories originally appearing in the *Strand Magazine,* December 1892–December 1893.

The Hound of the Baskervilles. London: George Newnes, 1902. Third Holmes novel, serialized in the *Strand Magazine,* August 1901–April 1902.

The Return of Sherlock Holmes. London: George Newnes, 1905. The third collection of short stories originally appearing in the *Strand Magazine,* October 1903–December 1904.

The Valley of Fear. London: Smith, Elder, 1915. Fourth Holmes novel, originally serialized in the *Strand Magazine,* September 1914–May 1915.

His Last Bow. London: John Murray, 1917. Fourth collection of short stories, including those originally serialized in the *Strand Magazine,* September 1908–September 1917, and "The Cardboard Box," January 1893.

The Case-Book of Sherlock Holmes. London: John Murray, 1927. Fifth and final collection of short stories that originally appeared in the *Strand Magazine*, October 1921–December 1926.

Holmes Collections

The Complete Sherlock Holmes Short Stories. London: John Murray, 1928. The standard English edition of the stories collected in the *Adventures*, the *Memoirs*, the *Return, His Last Bow*, and the *Case-book*.

The Complete Sherlock Holmes Long Stories. London: John Murray, 1929. The standard English edition of *A Study in Scarlet, The Sign of Four, The Hound of the Baskervilles*, and *The Valley of Fear*.

The Complete Sherlock Holmes. 2 vols. New York: Doubleday, 1930. The standard American edition of all 60 Sherlock Holmes fictions. Includes an introduction by the American Sherlockian Christopher Morley.

The Annotated Sherlock Holmes. 2 vols. Edited by William S. Baring-Gould. New York: Clarkson N. Potter, 1967. This Sherlockian collection of the complete Holmes fictions rearranges them in the order in which they "really occurred." In addition to much Sherlockian speculation about sources and biography, this also provides useful annotations on the stories' social and historical context.

Sherlock Holmes: The Complete Novels and Stories. 2 vols. New York: Bantam, 1986. Complete paperback Sherlock Holmes; with an introduction by Loren D. Estleman.

The Oxford Sherlock Holmes. 9 vols. Edited by Owen Dudley Edwards. Oxford and New York: Oxford University Press, 1993. Complete and extensively annotated series of Holmes novels and collected short stories; the *Adventures of Sherlock Holmes* volume features a useful introduction and notes by Richard Lancelyn Green.

Major Novels and Nonfiction (First English Editions)

Micah Clarke. London: Longmans, Green, 1889. Historical novel based on seventeenth-century Puritans.

The Firm of Girdlestone. London: Chatto and Windus, 1890. Doyle's first novel, a contemporary story set in Edinburgh.

The White Company. London: Smith, Elder, 1891. Chivalric novel set in the fourteenth century.

The Refugees. London: Longmans, Green, 1893. A historical novel tracing the adventures of Franco-Canadian Huguenots.

The Stark Munro Letters. London: Longmans, Green, 1895. Semiautobiographical novel about a young man's struggles with religious doubt.

Rodney Stone. London: Smith, Elder, 1896. Follows the adventures of a prizefighter in Regency England.

Selected Bibliography

The Exploits of Brigadier Gerard. London: George Newnes, 1896. Collection of stories based on the adventures of a Napoleonic soldier.

Uncle Bernac. London: Smith, Elder, 1897. Historical novel based on the Napoleonic wars.

The Tragedy of the Korosko. London: Smith, Elder, 1898. Adventure tale set in contemporary Egypt.

A Duet with an Occasional Chorus. London: Grant Richards, 1899. Contemporary love story.

The Great Boer War. London: Smith, Elder, 1900. History of the Boer War in South Africa.

Adventures of Gerard. London: George Newnes, 1903. Second series of stories following Doyle's fictional Napoleonic soldier.

Sir Nigel. London: Smith, Elder, 1906. A historical fiction set shortly before the events of *The White Company.*

Through the Magic Door. London: Smith, Elder, 1907. Doyle on reading and his favorite books.

The Lost World. London: Hodder and Stoughton, 1912. First novel following the science-fiction adventures of Professor Challenger.

The Poison Belt. London: Hodder and Stoughton, 1913. The second Professor Challenger fiction.

The British Campaign in France and Flanders. 6 vols. London: Hodder and Stoughton, 1916–20. History of World War I.

The New Revelation. London: Hodder and Stoughton, 1918. First of Doyle's treatises on spiritualism.

The Vital Message. London: Hodder and Stoughton, 1919. Second full-length work on spiritualism.

The History of Spiritualism. 2 vols. London: Cassell, 1926. Doyle's major work on spiritualism.

The Land of Mist. London: Hutchinson, 1926. Another Challenger adventure, in which the professor becomes a spiritualist.

Secondary Sources

Bibliographic Guides

Barzun, Jacques, and Wendell Hertig Taylor. *A Catalogue of Crime.* 1971. New York: Harper and Row, 1989. Selective and opinionated annotated bibliography of primary and secondary sources on crime fiction; listings on Holmes are less comprehensive and "fundamental" than claimed.

de Waal, Ronald Burt. *The World Bibliography of Sherlock Holmes and Dr. Watson.* New York: Bramball House, 1974. Covers primary sources, including stage and screen versions, and Sherlockian and other secondary sources through the early 1970s.

————. *The International Sherlock Holmes.* Hamden, Conn.: Archon Books, 1980. Updates *World Bibliography* through 1980.

Green, Richard Lancelyn, and John Michael Gibson. *A Bibliography of Arthur Conan Doyle.* Oxford: Clarendon Press, 1983. Comprehensive bibliography of all of Doyle's writings, including biographical and some critical commentaries on him.

Johnson, Timothy W., and Julia Johnson. *Crime Fiction Criticism: An Annotated Bibliography.* New York: Garland, 1981. Selected bibliography with descriptive annotations; includes a section on Sherlock Holmes.

Biographical and Autobiographical Materials

Carr, John Dickson. *The Life of Sir Arthur Conan Doyle.* New York: Harper and Brothers, 1949. Idealizing authorized biography. Although one of the few biographers given access to Doyle's letters and papers, Carr is sometimes misleading because of his tendency to fictionalize important episodes in Doyle's life.

Cox, J. Randolph. "Sir Arthur Conan Doyle." In *British Mystery Writers 1860–1919.* Edited by Bernard Benstock and Thomas F. Staley. Detroit: Gale Research, 1988, 112–34. Vol. 70 of *Dictionary of Literary Biography.* Overview of Doyle's literary career, including selected bibliography of primary and secondary sources.

Doyle, Adrian Conan. *The True Arthur Conan Doyle.* London: John Murray, 1945. In this rather defensive biography, Doyle's son attempts to redress the depreciation of his father's talents by Hesketh Pearson.

Doyle, Arthur Conan. *Memories and Adventures: The Autobiography of Sir Arthur Conan Doyle.* London: Hodder and Stoughton, 1924. Doyle's rather selective reminiscences about his life and work.

————. *Letters to the Press: The Unknown Conan Doyle.* Edited by John Michael Gibson and Richard Lancelyn Green. London: Secker and Warburg, 1986. Collected letters to the press by Doyle on various political and social issues from 1879–1930.

Edwards, Owen Dudley. *The Quest for Sherlock Holmes.* Totowa, N.J.: Barnes and Noble, 1983. Comprehensive study of Doyle's first 23 years and the ways they may have contributed to his literary work; the only biography to give full consideration to the possible influence of Charles Doyle's chronic alcoholism and mental debility on his son.

Selected Bibliography

Higham, Charles. *The Adventures of Conan Doyle: The Life of the Creator of Sherlock Holmes.* New York: Norton, 1976. First half of text gives extensive coverage to Sherlock Holmes in Doyle's career; see closing pages for an explanation of why many of the Doyle manuscripts and papers are currently inaccessible to the public.

Lamond, John. *Arthur Conan Doyle: A Memoir.* London: John Murray, 1931. This laudatory biography by a friend and fellow spiritualist stresses Doyle's involvement in that belief; includes an epilogue by Lady Jean Conan Doyle.

Lellenberg, Jon L., ed. *The Quest for Sir Arthur Conan Doyle: Thirteen Biographers in Search of a Life.* Carbondale: Southern Illinois University Press, 1987. Extremely helpful collection of essays assessing the major Doyle biographies and identifying central issues and problems among them.

Nordon, Pierre. *Conan Doyle: A Biography.* Translated by Frances Partridge. New York: Holt, Rinehart and Winston, 1967. Most reliable literary biography of Doyle; this English translation is somewhat shorter than original French version (*Sir Arthur Conan Doyle: L'Homme et l'oeuvre* [Paris: Didier, 1964]) and leaves out appendices containing various letters, reminiscences, and bibliographical information.

Orel, Harold, ed. *Sir Arthur Conan Doyle: Interviews and Recollections.* New York: St. Martin's, 1991. Reprints essays, newspaper profiles, interviews, and reminiscences by Doyle and people who knew him.

Pearsall, Ronald. *Conan Doyle: A Biographical Solution.* New York: St. Martin's, 1977. Belittling and at times imprecise biography, although useful for placing Doyle's attitudes and the Holmes character in the context of late Victorian concerns.

Pearson, Hesketh. *Conan Doyle: His Life and Art.* London: Methuen, 1943. Early biography that provoked Adrian Conan Doyle's rebuttal for portraying his father as a "man in the street"; includes one chapter devoted to Sherlock Holmes.

Sir Arthur Conan Doyle Centenary 1859–1959. London: John Murray, 1959. A celebration of Doyle's life and work, mainly through photographs and other memorabilia, much of it not published elsewhere. Includes short introductory assessments by Adrian Conan Doyle and Pierre Weil-Nordon.

Selected Sherlockian Interpretations

Baring-Gould, William. *Sherlock Holmes of Baker Street: A Life of the World's First Consulting Detective.* New York: Bramball House, 1962. A fictionalized Sherlockian biography of the famous sleuth.

Dakin, David Martin. *A Sherlock Holmes Commentary*. Newton Abbot, Eng.: David and Charles, 1972. Speculates on dating various stories and explaining various inconsistencies of detail in them.

Harrison, Michael. *The London of Sherlock Holmes*. Newton Abbot, Eng.: David and Charles, 1972. Sherlockian examination of London landmarks that figure in the Holmes canon.

————, ed. *Beyond Baker Street: A Sherlockian Anthology*. Indianapolis: Bobbs-Merrill, 1976. Classic Sherlockian essays on the canon, its adaptation by others, and Doyle's life.

Murphy, Cait. "The Game's Still Afoot." *Atlantic Monthly* (March 1987): 58–66. Balanced history of the Sherlockian tradition from its origins to the present.

Shreffler, Philip A., ed. *Sherlock Holmes by Gas-Lamp: Highlights from the First Four Decades of the Baker-Street Journal*. New York: Fordham University Press, 1989. Selected essays from the major Sherlockian journal.

Smith, Edgar W., ed. *Profile by Gaslight: An Irregular Reader about the Private Life of Sherlock Holmes*. New York: Simon and Schuster, 1944. Anthology of classic early Sherlockian essays by Vincent Starrett, Dorothy Sayers, Rex Stout, and others.

Starrett, Vincent. *The Private Life of Sherlock Holmes*. New York: Macmillan, 1933. Mainly a Sherlockian biography of Holmes, although also includes useful information about Doyle's creation of the character and its early publication history.

————, ed. *221B: Studies in Sherlock Holmes*. New York: Macmillan, 1940. Mostly Sherlockian treatments of Holmes, plus a few essays on him as a literary creation and an index of characters in the canon.

Books on Detective Fiction

Bloom, Clive, et al., eds. *Nineteenth-Century Suspense: From Poe to Conan Doyle*. New York: St. Martin's, 1988. Collection of analyses on mystery and suspense fiction that includes essays on Poe, Collins, Stoker, Doyle, and others.

Haycraft, Howard, ed. *The Life and Times of the Detective Story*. New York: Appleton-Century, 1941. History of detective fiction from the early nineteenth century; includes a chapter mainly on Sherlock Holmes.

————. *The Art of the Mystery Story*. New York: Simon and Schuster, 1946. Classic early essays on detective fiction.

Kayman, Martin A. *From Bow Street to Baker Street: Mystery, Detection, and Narrative*. New York: St. Martin's, 1992. Concerned with treatment of mystery in the development of detective fiction; includes useful background on the social and legal history that shaped changing types of the detective.

Knight, Stephen. *Form and Ideology in Crime Fiction*. Bloomington: Indiana University Press, 1980. Impact of ideology on the form and content of detective fiction from Newgate novel through the twentieth century; includes a chapter on Sherlock Holmes.

Landrum, Larry, Pat Browne, and Ray Browne, eds. *Dimensions of Detective Fiction*. n.p.: Popular Press, 1976. A collection of essays on the development of detective fiction.

Mandel, Ernest. *Delightful Murder: A Social History of the Crime Story*. London: Pluto Press, 1984. Marxist analysis of the relationship between capitalism and the development of crime fiction.

Moretti, Franco. *Signs Taken for Wonders: Essays in the Sociology of Literary Form*. Translated by Susan Fischer, David Forgacs, and David Miller. London: Verso, 1983. Chap. 5, "Clues," takes a penetrating look at the ideological assumptions embodied by the formal conventions of detective fiction.

Most, Glenn, and William Stowe, eds. *The Poetics of Murder*. San Diego: Harcourt Brace Jovanovich, 1983. Best recent anthology of theoretical approaches to detective fiction, from psychoanalytic to deconstructive.

Murch, Alma. *The Development of the Detective Novel*. New York: Greenwood Press, 1958. The most comprehensive history of crime fiction, from its roots through the twentieth century.

Ousby, Ian. *Bloodhounds of Heaven: The Detective in English Fiction from Godwin to Doyle*. Cambridge, Mass.: Harvard University Press, 1976. Analyzes social concerns that shaped detection and the detective from the nineteenth century through the early twentieth; includes a useful discussion of the evolution of the Holmes character over the course of time.

Panek, LeRoy L. *An Introduction to the Detective Story*. Bowling Green, Ohio: Bowling Green State University Popular Press, 1987. History of detective fiction in England and America; chapter on Doyle stresses literary influences on the Sherlock Holmes character.

Petersen, Audrey. *Victorian Masters of Mystery: From Wilkie Collins to Conan Doyle*. New York: Ungar, 1984. Traces history of the mystery story through major nineteenth-century writers; includes a chapter on Doyle and Holmes.

Porter, Dennis. *The Pursuit of Crime: Art and Ideology in Detective Fiction*. New Haven, Conn.: Yale University Press, 1981. Noteworthy for its analysis of the characteristic formal traits of detective fiction; insightful chapter on class issues in the evolution of the detective type.

Priestman, Martin. *Detective Fiction and Literature: The Figure on the Carpet.* New York: St. Martin's, 1991. Compares the form and effects of detective fiction to those of high-culture texts; provides a useful classification and analysis of the sources of crime in the Holmes stories.

Symons, Julian. *Bloody Murder: From the Detective Story to the Crime Novel.* 1972. Rev. ed., New York: Viking, 1985. History of the crime fiction from its French roots through the twentieth century, including a short chapter on Sherlock Holmes.

Todorov, Tzvetan. "The Typology of Detective Fiction." In *The Poetics of Prose.* Translated by Richard Howard, 42–52. Ithaca, N.Y.: Cornell University Press, 1971. Important formal analysis of the narrative structure of detective fictions.

Winks, Robin, ed. *Detective Fiction: A Collection of Critical Essays.* Englewood Cliffs, N.J.: Prentice-Hall, 1980. Anthology of central essays on detective fiction by authors such as Dorothy Sayers, W. H. Auden, Edmund Wilson, and others.

Books on Doyle or Holmes

Accardo, Pasquale. *Diagnosis and Detection: The Medical Iconography of Sherlock Holmes.* Rutherford, N.J.: Fairleigh Dickinson University Press, 1987. Evaluates claims about Holmes's scientific reasoning and examines literary archetypes suggested by the Holmes canon.

Bullard, Scott R., and Michael Leo Collins. *Who's Who in Sherlock Holmes.* New York: Taplinger, 1980. Mainly a dictionary of names and places, although also includes collated lists of quotations from the Holmes canon on selected topics (e.g., Holmes on music, Holmes on his methods of detection, etc.).

Costello, Peter. *The Real World of Sherlock Holmes: The True Crimes Investigated by Arthur Conan Doyle.* New York: Carroll and Graf, 1991. Examines Doyle's involvement in investigating actual crimes.

Cox, Don Richard. *Arthur Conan Doyle.* New York: Frederick Ungar, 1985. Short study of Doyle's life and literary career, including summaries of his major works.

Eco, Umberto, and Thomas A. Sebeok, eds. *The Sign of Three: Dupin, Holmes, Peirce.* Bloomington: Indiana University Press, 1983. Important collection of essays on semiotic issues raised by Holmesian detection and its connections to the work of American philosopher Charles Peirce.

Eyles, Allen. *Sherlock Holmes: A Centenary Celebration.* New York: Harper and Row, 1986. Traces the publication history of Sherlock Holmes, including stage and screen versions; extensively illustrated.

Green, Richard Lancelyn, ed. *The Uncollected Sherlock Holmes.* Harmonds-

Selected Bibliography

worth, Eng.: Penguin, 1983. Includes a useful selection of prefaces, reviews, parodies, and other Holmes-related materials, preceded by Green's detailed publication history of the Holmes canon.

―――, ed. *The Sherlock Holmes Letters*. London: Secker and Warburg, 1986. Chronicles the life of Sherlock Holmes in the public press through letters to the editor, press notices, contests, and the like. Green's long and useful introduction provides a history of responses to the Sherlock Holmes phenomenon.

Haining, Peter, ed. *A Sherlock Holmes Compendium*. London: Unwin, 1980. Useful collection of essays, letters, parodies, and other materials inspired by Holmes.

Hall, Trevor H. *Sherlock Holmes and His Creator*. New York: St. Martin's, 1977. In addition to some Sherlockian pieces, includes essays on the literary influence of Holmes and on Doyle's involvement with spiritualism.

Hardwick, Michael. *The Complete Guide to Sherlock Holmes*. London: Weidenfeld and Nicolson, 1986. Excerpts, plot summaries, and indexes of characters for the entire canon.

Harrison, Michael. *A Study in Surmise: The Making of Sherlock Holmes*. Bloomington, Ind.: Gaslight Publications, 1984. Considers possible sources in Doyle's life and times for the Sherlock Holmes stories.

Herbert, Paul D. *The Sincerest Form of Flattery: A Historical Survey of Parodies, Pastiches and Other Imitative Writings of Sherlock Holmes, 1891–1980*. Bloomington, Ind.: Gaslight Publications, 1983. Extensive collection of writings imitating and inspired by Holmes.

Jaffe, Jacqueline. *Arthur Conan Doyle*. Boston: Twayne, 1987. Study of Doyle's life and work, including several chapters on Sherlock Holmes.

Klinefelter, Walter. *Sherlock Holmes in Portrait and Profile*. New York: Schocken, 1975. Comprehensive survey of illustrations for the Holmes stories.

Orel, Harold, ed. *Critical Essays on Sir Arthur Conan Doyle*. New York: G. K. Hall, 1992. A selection of essays on various aspects of Doyle's literary career; reprints recent journal articles and excerpts of books by such scholars as Clausen, Barolsky, Knight, Accardo, A. Jaffe, and others.

Pointer, Michael. *The Public Life of Sherlock Holmes*. Newton Abbot, Eng.: David and Charles, 1975. Focuses mainly on stage and screen versions of Holmes and includes an extensive catalog of performances.

Redmond, Christopher. *In Bed with Sherlock Holmes: Sexual Elements in Arthur Conan Doyle's Stories of the Great Detective*. Toronto: Simon and Pierre, 1984. Analyzes sexual behavior and gender issues in the light of Victorian mores and attitudes.

Redmond, Donald A. *Sherlock Holmes: A Study in Sources*. Kingston, Ont.:

McGill-Queen's University Press, 1982. Exhaustive survey of possible sources in Doyle's life for people and events in the Holmes stories.

————. *Sherlock Holmes among the Pirates: Copyright and Conan Doyle in America, 1890–1930*. New York: Greenwood, 1990. Publishing history and bibliography of Sherlock Holmes stories in the United States; major emphasis on the fate of *The Sign of Four* and *A Study in Scarlet* in the days before international copyright protection.

Rosenberg, Samuel. *Naked Is the Best Disguise: The Death and Resurrection of Sherlock Holmes*. Indianapolis: Bobbs-Merrill, 1974. Analysis of the ways the Holmes stories reveal Doyle's personal neuroses; undercut by its inaccuracies in the facts of Doyle's life and its highly speculative reasoning.

Shreffler, Philip A., ed. *The Baker Street Reader: Cornerstone Writings about Sherlock Holmes*. Westport, Conn.: Greenwood Press, 1984. Significant literary tributes by writers such as Vincent Starrett, T. S. Eliot, Edmund Wilson, and others; also includes some classic Sherlockian essays.

Tracy, Jack W. *The Encyclopedia Sherlockiana*. Garden City, N.Y.: Doubleday, 1977. Dictionary of names, places, and objects, both fictional and historical, in the Holmes canon.

Essays on Holmes

Barolsky, Paul. "The Case of the Domesticated Aesthete." *Virginia Quarterly Review* 60, no. 3 (1984): 438–52. Thoroughly traces parallels between Holmes and the late-nineteenth-century figure of the aesthete.

Clausen, Christopher. "Sherlock Holmes, Order, and the Late Victorian Mind." *Georgia Review* 38 (1984): 104–23. Usefully situates Holmes's attitudes toward crime and detection in the context of late Victorian concerns about intellectual and social order.

Hall, Jasmine Yong. "Ordering the Sensational: Sherlock Holmes and the Female Gothic." *Studies in Short Fiction* 28 (1991): 295–303. Relates Doyle's treatment of women to Gothic traditions, focusing on "The Speckled Band" and other stories.

Hennessy, Rosemary, and Rajeswari Mohan. "The Construction of Woman in Three Popular Texts of Empire: Towards a Critique of Materialist Feminism." *Textual Practice* 3, no. 3 (1989): 323–59. Considers the treatment of women in "The Speckled Band" as it relates to larger issues of gender, colonialism, and patriarchy.

Hodgson, John A. "The Recoil of 'The Speckled Band': Detective Story and Detective Discourse." *Poetics Today* 13 (Summer 1992): 309–24. A deconstructive reading that considers the ways this story violates the laws of the detective-story genre.

Selected Bibliography

Jaffe, Audrey. "Detecting the Beggar: Arthur Conan Doyle, Henry Mayhew, and 'The Man with the Twisted Lip.'" *Representations* 31 (1990): 96–117. Considers this story in the context of Victorian assumptions about work and middle-class identity.

Jann, Rosemary. "Sherlock Holmes Codes the Social Body." *ELH* 57 (1990): 685–708. An examination of the ideological issues raised by Holmes's claims to predict and identify social identity throughout the canon.

Kissane, James, and John Kissane. "Sherlock Holmes and the Ritual of Reason." *Nineteenth-Century Fiction* 17 (1963): 353–62. Historical analysis of attitudes toward reason and superstition, focusing on *The Hound of the Baskervilles*.

McConnell, Frank. "Detecting Order amid Disorder." *Wilson Quarterly* 11, no. 2 (1987): 172–83. Analyzes the myth of reason developed by the Holmes canon and places it in historical perspective.

Van Dover, J. K. "The Lens and the Violin: Sherlock Holmes and the Rescue of Science." *Clues* 9, no. 2 (1988): 37–51. Convincing analysis of the way the Holmes character served to rehabilitate the scientist by quieting Victorian fears about the potentially revolutionary threats posed by scientific reasoning.

Index

147

Index

The Author

Rosemary Jann has received degrees from Duke University and Northwestern University. She has taught at Ripon College and Rutgers University and is currently professor and chair of English at George Mason University. She is the author of *The Art and Science of Victorian History*, and her articles on Victorian literature and intellectual history have appeared in journals such as *Victorian Studies*, *English Literary History*, and *Texas Studies in Literature and Language*.